SCENES FROM THE PAST :

THE
MID WALES
LINE

MOAT LANE JUNCTION TO BRECON VIA LLANIDLOES, RHAYADER, BUILTH WELLS AND TALYLLYN JUNCTION.

DEREK J. LOWE

(*Above*) The new 'second' Llanidloes station building was open for business in 1864, (the 'old' original L&N station, about 250 yards to the north east, was then used as a coal and ore yard). The building was certainly a very imposing structure and at the time gave the Cambrian a strong dominance in the area.

Photograph: G. J. Biddle

(*Above*) Viewed from the footplate of BR No.46516 and looking towards Moat Lane, the goods shed is to the left with the two road engine shed on the right. The latter could store four 'Mickey Mouse' BR 2-6-0's undercover. The loco coal road is extreme right. A gas lamp and GWR signs stand sentinel at the end of the island platform. May 1962.

Photograph: The late N. Jones/D. J. Lowe Archive

(*Above*) Llandinam station had a single platform with passing loop and small shunt facility by the 1950's. The building was rendered in a pleasant cream colour which complemented the brown ornate barge boards. There was a covered ground frame adjacent to the main building which was still used up to 1967 when the station yard was used for storing building supplies for the Clywedog dam construction. The village was made famous as the birth-place of David Davies, the railway contractor, colliery owner and MP. A statue (picture left) stands near to the station which can also be seen (below) from a train carriage taken in 1962.

Photographs : (*Above*) P. Fisher Collection (*centre and below*) D. J. Lowe Archive

The Mid Wales Line …... a brief history from Construction up to British Railways

Railway development in mid Wales was a little slow at first in getting started, that is if one compares it with those new lines that had been constructed in England by the end of the 1850's. There were some lines built in South Wales and along the North Wales coast by 1852 but within the confines of these two lines and the North and West route from Cardiff to Chester, (finally completed in 1854), there was a huge area devoid of railways. This state of affairs was not to last however, and by the mid 1860's a massive transformation was to have taken place. Business and Commerce were the main motivators for opening up this part of Wales, with many leading businessmen keen to invest and with some aspiring to having a seat on the Boards of these new railway companies.

Two companies taking a keen interest in railway development in the late 1850's were the Mid Wales Railway (MWR), and the Manchester and Milford Railway (M&MR). They were watching carefully how their near railway 'neighbours' developments were progressing, and that their endeavours would soon see them merging into the new Cambrian Railways (Cam.R). Meanwhile, the Mid Wales Railway had aspirations of tapping into the New York passenger traffic emanating from Milford Haven in South West Wales, and of developing branch lines westwards across mid Wales to Aberystwyth. They would ultimately fall short of their ambitions but more of this later. Meanwhile, the M&MR had visions of a diagonal line running across Wales, through the mountains via Llangurig, to link up with their line north of Carmarthen at Pencader and so form a main route from South West Wales to Manchester and the lucrative cotton mills of Lancashire. Both companies would make end on connections at Llanidloes and envisaged agreeing running powers over the new Cambrian Railways for markets in England and beyond. However it would be one of the pre Cambrian constituent companies that would dictate their future progress for now, and that was the Llanidloes and Newtown Railway (L&NR).

The Llanidloes and Newtown would be the first to get their trains running, (30th April 1859 for Goods with Passenger traffic following on 31st August 1859), but because neighbouring lines had not been completed it was left somewhat isolated at first! The situation would change very quickly over the next five years by which time the neighbouring small railway companies, namely the Oswestry and Newtown Railway (O&NR), the Newtown and Machynlleth Railway (N&MR), the Oswestry, Ellesmere and Whitchurch Railway (OE&WR), the Aberystwyth and Welsh Coast Railway (A&WCR) along with the Llanidloes and Newtown Railway, would be incorporated into the Cambrian Railways (Cam.R) from 5th July 1865. Other main players included the Great Western Railway Railway (GWR) along with the London and North Western Railway (LNWR) with their joint line from Shrewsbury to Buttington Junction (opened on 27th January 1862). With the future prospects of a system of lines in place such as these and with permissions agreed for running powers, one can understand the great aspirations companies like the Mid Wales and the Manchester and Milford had for their share holders at the end of the 1850's and early 1860's.

The Mid Wales Railway Act of Parliament for a railway from Llanidloes to Newbridge was passed on 1st August 1859, with the first sod being cut near Rhayader on the 2nd September 1859. It would be one of many railways Acts it placed before Parliament for various lines and branches, including one to Aberystwyth via Rhayader. Around this time the Manchester and Milford Railway had also presented a Railway Act for it's line from Llanidloes to Pencader via Llangurig. When both Acts were passed, Parliament failed to note that both were on the same route for about one and half miles! Construction would have been difficult for two companies building on the same area of land, and when a stalemate resulted with neither company accepting the others proposals, the Llanidloes and Newtown Railway stepped in to build the line for them. The Act that enabled this arrangement forbade the L&N to work over its own line, but it was allowed to collect five percent of the capital cost in rent. A new joint station was constructed in Llanidloes with locomotive and goods facilities and the two independent lines (the

MWR and the M&MR) ran southwards from the station for approximately one and half miles to Penpontbren 'junction' by the Dulas River. Note the lines did not connect with each other, but it was at this location that effectively the two lines met the Cambrian (as the L&NR was soon to become). The branch to Llangurig was built by the M&MR but the continuation through a long tunnel and on to Pencader was never undertaken, the company eventually realising the expense and the difficulty of the undertaking. The short link between Penpontbren and Llangurig was abandoned by 1865. Instead, the M&MR went northwards with its west Wales line from Pencader and decided on a route to Aberystwyth via Trawscoed instead.

We should appreciate then that the northern point where the Mid Wales Railway started from, was not at Llanidloes, but in a quiet, lonely spot, on the side of a hill beside the waters of the Dulas River in the Cambrian mountains.... perhaps not such a bad spot after all.

(*Above*) Tylwch Halt looking in the up direction towards Moat Lane Junction. The surrounding terrain giving some idea of the problems the Mid Wales Railway had to encounter when constructing the line. It was forced to bridge and cross over many rivers on its journey through the mountains.   **Photograph**: P. Fisher Collection

Construction of the line by the MWR therefore started in this northerly backwater and spread in a southerly direction requiring much rock cutting to be carried out, especially near Tylwch, with a brick lined tunnel at Gilfach (Marteg) further south, situated in the valley of the Dulas river. The need to cross the rivers Dulas, Marteg, Ithon and Wye, sometimes on several ocassions for each river, added to the lines building costs. Some bridges were made up from standard cast-iron pillars with interlaced cross bracing. This was cheap and effective, but the downside to this method of construction meant that the weight of locomotives would be restricted. Despite additional strengthening years later using encased concrete supports, this weight restriction would always limit the line to the types of locomotives it would be allowed to use.

The local topography dictated passage of the railway slightly to the west of Rhayader via a very impressive embankment, at the base of which now flowed another river, the Wye. Further excavations to the south of the town required a short tunnel to be made before the railway was allowed to hug the river Wye down to the village of Doldowlod and on to Newbridge-on-Wye.

(*Above*) The front view of the Main Building at Llanidloes taken from the station approaches in the mid 1950's. Built as a principle station to serve three potentially independent railways, namely the L&NR (Cambrian), MWR, and the MMR of the 1860's, its status clearly declined as the years rolled by.
Photograph: P. Fisher Collection

(*Above and Left*) The 'second' Llanidloes station just after closure and included to assist potential modellers! The 'first ' station (to the NE of the goods yard) was dispensed with in 1864 but the tracks were used as a small coal and ore yard until closed and completely severed by 1928. The station building seen here has fortunately been saved and is used today for business use.
Photographs: D. J. Lowe Archive

REST DAY

(*Left*) A Sunday morning finds four BR Moguls on shed at Llanidloes depot, with No.46515 sticking its nose out! The line was dominated by these engines once the old Dean Goods and former Cambrian 0-6-0's were displaced in the early/mid 1950's, right up until closure of the line at the end of 1962. **Photograph**: D. J. Lowe Archive

(*Centre*) Llanidloes Signal Box c1959, showing all of the classic Cambrian traits of such a structure. **Photograph**: P. Fisher Collection

(*Below*) The south western end of Llanidloes station clearly shows the redundant former South Signal Box on the left (closed 1st Feb 1929). The public footbridge spanned all of the railway property with access to the island platform via a small ticket hut at the top of the steps! Coaching stock was usually shunted in platform three and stored for longer periods in the adjacent loop as indicated.
Photograph: D. J. Lowe Archive

In the 1930's, the GWR were keen to cater for the ever growing tourist market, by building additional halts on its lines. It scattered many on the Cambrian Coast and was eager to do the same on the Mid Wales. Considerations had to be made as to their locations, as drivers would not be too enthralled having to pull up and restart a train from a halt on an incline! Even so, short platforms were built at Llangorse Lake, Glan-yr-Afon (siding), and especially for that new breed of outside walker, the hiker, at Marteg, Llanstephan and Llanfaredd. Great efforts were made to stimulate traffic at this time on the line. Agricultural shows in Brecon, the Radnorshire Show, and even the Shrewsbury Flower Fete saw several trains organised to visit these events. Likewise, day excursion trips were run for example from Builth Wells to Liverpool and one went from Llanidloes to Barry Island. They proved to be well patronised. Other trips from Llanidloes to Weston-super-Mare and return could be a little tiring to say the least, with an enduring twenty two and a half hours round trip starting at 5.30am the previous day! Tourism was of great importance, not only to the railway but equally important to the many Bed and Breakfast establishments, scattered through the many small towns and villages along the course of the railway.

Goods traffic had always been of a mixed nature. Obvious 'local' trade was in the livestock and agricultural business and timber was taken from several private sidings for cutting and exporting to the coal and building industries. There were several quarries including Llanelwedd near Builth Wells which moved vast quantities of stone for road use and from North Wales slate was moved via the Mid Wales line to South Wales. A regular train carried Dolomite from Llynclys Quarry for years to the Iron and Steel industry at Ebbw Vale, and Dowlais. Household needs came to the area via the railway such as coal, oil, and foodstuffs along with fertilisers for the farming industry.

The trusty Dean Goods engines were still the mainstay of the line but the odd small 0-4-2 tank engine of the 48XX class were noted on Mid Wales trains around the 1935 period. Likewise the appearance of a few lightweight 0-6-0 Pannier Tanks were recorded, but the prospects of any new locomotives coming to the line were virtually nil at this time. The new Collett 22XX 0-6-0 tender engines now encrouching onto the northern sections of the 'Cambrian' were far to heavy for the old Mid Wales.

The Second World War did not really affect the line quite so much as in the first, in fact it was fairly quiet. Some of the Dean Goods engines were requisitioned by the army to serve abroad, and some would never return. There were no 'Jellicoe' specials this time, but who knows whether the old Mid Wales line might have seen the odd military train carrying something special, perhaps of the likes carried by the 'Saltney Goods' munitions trains up to Aberystwyth via the former M&MR!

After WWII the GWR along with the other members making up the Big Four, were nationalised from the 1st January 1948. Our railway line running down through the very heart of Wales would now move into the British Railways era and be part of the Western Region. The additional route mileage from Moat Lane Junction to Llanidloes and the line onwards to Brecon would embody the original name of the company that built most of it, such that years later railwaymen would often refer to it as .... The Mid Wales Line.

We are now ready to follow the lines last fourteen years of operation under the British Railways banner. This would see the eventual retirement of the Dean Goods engines, the introduction of a new class of 2-6-0 locomotive, before closure of the line would come at the end of 1962. Starting from Moat Lane Junction I trust you will enjoy your journey!

Gradient Profile for the Moat Lane Junction to Brecon Railway Line

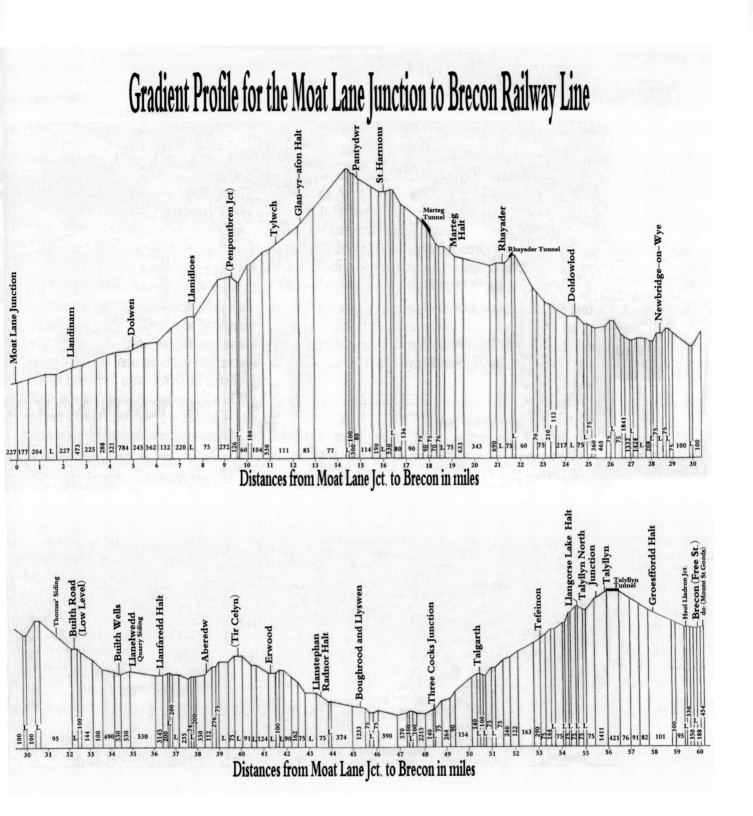

Distances from Moat Lane Jct. to Brecon in miles

Distances from Moat Lane Jct. to Brecon in miles

The reader should be aware that the above distances quoted above are set from Moat Lane Junction as the datum, and correspond to the information provided in the Working Timetable (WTT). Note that the WTT also provided distance information from Whitchurch. For the point of clarity, this has not been included on the above profiles.

Footnote: Names of stations, towns and villages used in this book are spelt in such a way as to be contemporary with the date of the photograph, map or timetable.

(*Above*) Another northbound train, this time just south of Glan yr Afon Halt. The halt is just beyond the road over bridge in the distance and around the bend. Once again the Afon Dulas crosses just in front of the engine and heads eastwards before swinging northwards for the railway to cross it once again before entering Glan yr afon. The rise left of centre is Graig-iar at 1339 feet. May 1962

Photograph: The late N. Jones/D. J. Lowe Archive

PENPONTBREN JUNCTION

(Left) The bridge that used to take the ex.MMR line to Llangurig and deviating from the ex MWR line, as seen from a passing train in 1962. Divergence occurred one and a half miles south of Llanidloes South Signal Box. The ex MMR line did for a short time make a proper junction connection in 1872 but the branch was removed in 1882, as was the junction. **Photograph**: D. J. Lowe Archive

(*Above*) The wonderful scenery associated with the Mid Wales line is clearly exemplified in this view. An Ivatt class 2 with three coaches makes its way into Tylwch station (just the other side of the bridge) on an up train in the mid 1950's. The ex GWR coaching stock would have been in 'blood and custard' at this time with the engine being relatively new.
Photograph: P. Fisher Collection

(*Above*) Dean Goods No.2452 backs down onto Moat Lane loco shed for servicing on the 14th July 1952. The fireman walks on ahead to select the appropriate road. The engine managed to survive until the October when it was withdrawn from service. Note the public footpath on the right which went through the loco yard!
Photograph: D. J. Lowe Archive

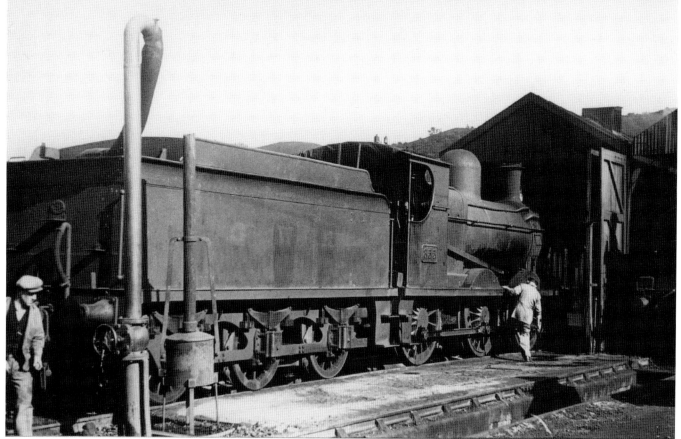

(*Above*) Ex Cambrian '15' class 0-6-0 No.855, and perhaps not surprisingly still showing 'GWR' on its tender at this date of 9th September 1949, is checked over in the small engine shed at Moat Lane. Although initially the class were considered to be too heavy for the Mid Wales line they were frequent visitors especially after WWII.
Photograph: D. J. Lowe Archive

(*Above*) No.2409 this time seen leaving Moat Lane Junction with the 5.30 pm passenger for Brecon on 14th July 1952. Note Moat Lane North Signal Box on the left of picture.
Photograph: D. J. Lowe Archive

MOAT LANE DEPARTUES

(*Below*) Ten years later we see BR Class 2 No.46518 at the head of the 12.27 pm service to Llanidloes. This would take 17 minutes for the 7¾ miles including stops at Llandinam and Dolwen Halt if required.
Photograph: The late Colin Caddy

(*Above*) About half a mile south of Pantydwr we have now picked up the Afon Marteg which can be seen on the right. In the far distance the line curves to the right where we will soon call by St Harmons. Note the bleak nature of the surroundings now.
Photograph: The late N. Jones/D. J. Lowe Archive

(*Above*) We arrive in St Harmons station and this view, looking north east, with the crossing gates open reveals the small siding that was present here. It was initially used for lime traffic and then general goods until the line was closed.
                                                                                    Photograph: D. J. Lowe Collection

BR (WR) Pantydwr
(late 1950's)

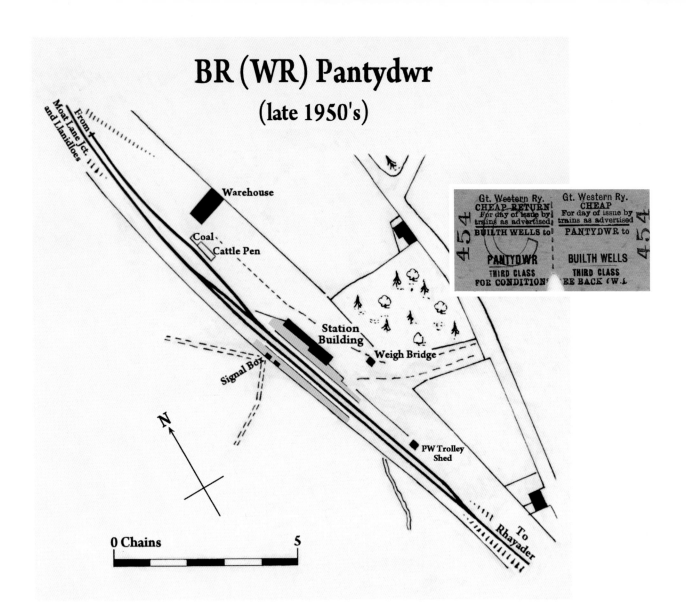

From Moat Lane Jct. and Llanidloes

Warehouse

Coal

Cattle Pen

Station Building

Signal Box

Weigh Bridge

N

PW Trolley Shed

To Rhayader

0 Chains   5

Gt. Western Ry.
CHEAP RETURN
For day of issue by
trains as advertised
BUILTH WELLS to
PANTYDWR
THIRD CLASS
FOR CONDITION

Gt. Western Ry.
CHEAP
For day of issue by
trains as advertised
PANTYDWR to
BUILTH WELLS
THIRD CLASS
EE BACK (W.)

454

454

(*left*) Pantydwr station was not only the highest point on the Mid Wales Line, but was the highest point on the entire Cambrian system at 947 feet. Having two platforms and a small yard to the north it was a rest and be thankful spot for engine crews approaching from either direction! The climb from Llanidloes was pretty relentless with only a primary stop at Tylwch and a 'hindrance' stop at Glan-yr-Afon for the driver! Gradients of 1 in 60, 75, 77, and 85 would be encountered. The southerly approach was not much better. The line would have been climbing virtually all the way from Three Cocks Junction (some 35 miles away!), interspersed with admittedly several stops and some downhill sections, but the section from Rhayader to Pantydwr had a fearsome seven miles of stiff gradients including sections of 1 in 60 and several at 1 in 75! **Photograph**: D. J. Lowe Collection

(*Above*) Approaching Moat Lane (in the far distance) from the South West. The crossing with the outer Home signal pulled off is the near site of the original L&N Caersws station.
Photograph: The late N. Jones/D. J. Lowe Archive

(*Right*) Just outside Llandinam station was Afon Hafren viaduct which spanned the River Severn. It was 64 yards long and pictured here from the main A492 road. The station is just off to the left of this view.
Photograph: D. J. Lowe Archive

(*Above*) Llandinam station had a single platform with passing loop and small shunt facility by the 1950's. The building was rendered in a pleasant cream colour which complemented the brown ornate barge boards. There was a covered ground frame adjacent to the main building which was still used up to 1967 when the station yard was used for storing building supplies for the Clywedog dam construction. The village was made famous as the birth-place of David Davies, the railway contractor, colliery owner and MP. A statue (picture left) stands near to the station which can also be seen (below) from a train carriage taken in 1962.

Photographs : (*Above*) P. Fisher Collection (*centre and below*) D. J. Lowe Archive

DOLWEN HALT

(*Above*) Dolwen Halt was built almost identical to Llandinam. The word 'Halt' seems to have been added as a post war addition. It originally had a small signal box (c1890) but this was removed in 1910 to serve at Borth on the Coast. A ground frame was then utilised, eventually being removed along with the loop and sidings on 28th November 1956. A late 1950's view.
Photograph: The late J. Fozard/S. Fozard

(*Below*) About one mile west of, and heading towards Dolwen Halt, with a train for Moat Lane Junction. The River Severn is on the right. Note the 'Termination' of speed restriction sign and the PW trolley refuge siding a few yards beyond on the right. A 1962 view.
Photograph: The late N. Jones/D. J. Lowe Archive

BR (WR) Llanidloes
(late 1950's)

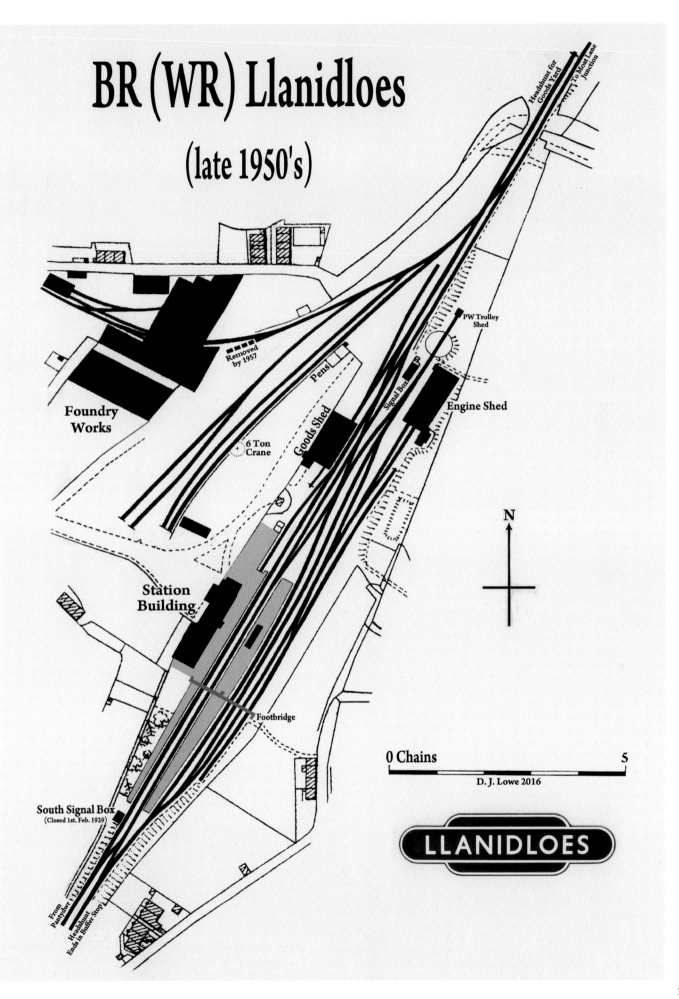

Headshunt for Goods Yard

To Moat Lane Junction

PW Trolley Shed

Removed by 1957

Pens

Signal Box

Engine Shed

Foundry Works

Goods Shed

6 Ton Crane

N

Station Building

Footbridge

0 Chains 5

D. J. Lowe 2016

South Signal Box
(Closed 1st. Feb. 1929)

From Pantydwr

Headshunt Ends in Buffer Stop

LLANIDLOES

(*Above*) The new 'second' Llanidloes station building was open for business in 1864, (the 'old' original L&N station, about 250 yards to the north east, was then used as a coal and ore yard). The building was certainly a very imposing structure and at the time gave the Cambrian a strong dominance in the area.   **Photograph**: G. J. Biddle

(*Above*) Viewed from the footplate of BR No.46516 and looking towards Moat Lane, the goods shed is to the left with the two road engine shed on the right. The latter could store four 'Mickey Mouse' BR 2-6-0's undercover. The loco coal road is extreme right. A gas lamp and GWR signs stand sentinel at the end of the island platform. May 1962.   **Photograph**: The late N. Jones/D. J. Lowe Archive

REST DAY

(*Left*) A Sunday morning finds four BR Moguls on shed at Llanidloes depot, with No.46515 sticking its nose out! The line was dominated by these engines once the old Dean Goods and former Cambrian 0-6-0's were displaced in the early/mid 1950's, right up until closure of the line at the end of 1962. **Photograph**: D. J. Lowe Archive

(*Centre*) Llanidloes Signal Box c1959, showing all of the classic Cambrian traits of such a structure. **Photograph**: P. Fisher Collection

(*Below*) The south western end of Llanidloes station clearly shows the redundant former South Signal Box on the left (closed 1st Feb 1929). The public footbridge spanned all of the railway property with access to the island platform via a small ticket hut at the top of the steps! Coaching stock was usually shunted in platform three and stored for longer periods in the adjacent loop as indicated.
Photograph: D. J. Lowe Archive

(*Above*) Mogul No.46516 stands in the up platform with a train from Brecon to Moat Lane in 1962. Note the original MWR water column to the right and the classic platform bay window to the main station building. On the island platform to the left can be seen the wooden built Waiting Room erected in the early 1950's.   **Photograph**: The late J. Fozard/S. Fozard

(*Above*) A view of the above service from the southern end of the station. The striking resemblance of the station building at Llanidloes to that at Oswestry and Ellesmere is most apparent. Note that there were no platform canopies at Llanidloes. The goods shed warehouse may be seen in the distance where there was also the goods yard and the private foundry of J. Mills & Co.

Photograph: The late J. Fozard/S. Fozard

(*Above*) A view from the steps of the footbridge at Llanidloes of a Brecon to Moat Lane train in the late 1950's at the up platform. The Station Master is supervising proceedings as friends say their goodbyes in the first coach. The attached covered van on the right has the station 'Aberystwyth' chalked on the sliding door, so presumeably this will be dropped off at Moat Lane for forwarding on. A combination of Western Region stock and ex LMS stock stored in platform three can be seen in this view.

Photograph: P. Fisher Collection

(*Above*) The front view of the Main Building at Llanidloes taken from the station approaches in the mid 1950's. Built as a principle station to serve three potentially independent railways, namely the L&NR (Cambrian), MWR, and the MMR of the 1860's, its status clearly declined as the years rolled by.
Photograph: P. Fisher Collection

(*Above and Left*) The 'second' Llanidloes station just after closure and included to assist potential modellers! The 'first ' station (to the NE of the goods yard) was dispensed with in 1864 but the tracks were used as a small coal and ore yard until closed and completely severed by 1928. The station building seen here has fortunately been saved and is used today for business use.
Photographs: D. J. Lowe Archive

PENPONTBREN JUNCTION

(Left) The bridge that used to take the ex.MMR line to Llangurig and deviating from the ex MWR line, as seen from a passing train in 1962. Divergence occurred one and a half miles south of Llanidloes South Signal Box. The ex MMR line did for a short time make a proper junction connection in 1872 but the branch was removed in 1882, as was the junction.   **Photograph**: D. J. Lowe Archive

(*Above*) The wonderful scenery associated with the Mid Wales line is clearly exemplified in this view. An Ivatt class 2 with three coaches makes its way into Tylwch station (just the other side of the bridge) on an up train in the mid 1950's. The ex GWR coaching stock would have been in 'blood and custard' at this time with the engine being relatively new.
                                                                                          Photograph: P. Fisher Collection

TYLWCH
HALT

(*Right*) Ivatt class 2 2-6-0 No.46520 prepares to leave Tylwch Halt and head northwards with a service from Brecon. The locomotive bears an 89D shed code plate on the smokebox door indicating she is still under Oswestry's allocation, but was more than likely sub-shedded to either Moat Lane, Llanidloes or Brecon in this summer 1961 view.
Photograph: P. Fisher Collection

(*left*) Some rationalisation took place at Tylwch in the early 1950's. In this view looking northwards, we can see that the down line (on the right) has been removed. Likewise the trailing siding off the up line to the north of the station was also taken out. These changes took place on 20th December 1953. Tylwch signal box used to be sited just to the north of the up platform (see page 5) but this was removed during the September of 1953. In this c1957 view, the PW trolley refuge siding is still in place.
Photograph: P. Fisher Collection

(*Above left*) Passing through Tylwch northwards showing the down line intact. The up trailing siding can just be seen infront of Cambrian 0-6-0 No.855, Sept 1949. **Photograph**: The late H.C.Casserley/R.M Casserley.

(*Above right*) The rock cutting immediately to the south of the station. **Photograph**: P. Fisher Collection

(*Above*) South of Tylwch on a train heading northwards. The Afon Dulas is to the right with Old Chapel Hill (at 1398 feet high) directly infront of the straight railway track. This location is about half a mile to the north west of our next picture Glan yr Afon. May 1962
Photograph: D. J. Lowe Archive

(*Above*) Glan yr Afon Halt was opened on 16th January 1928 although a siding existed here long before this (1875!). It was situated just to the north of the platform. The siding served agricultural needs mainly fertiliser supplies etc but was removed in 1960. The photographer seems to have left his bicycle on the platform in this view looking towards Tylwch! **Photograph**: D. J. Lowe Collection

(*Above*) Another northbound train, this time just south of Glan yr Afon Halt. The halt is just beyond the road over bridge in the distance and around the bend. Once again the Afon Dulas crosses just in front of the engine and heads eastwards before swinging northwards for the railway to cross it once again before entering Glan yr afon. The rise left of centre is Graig-iar at 1339 feet. May 1962

Photograph: The late N. Jones/D. J. Lowe Archive

BR (WR) Pantydwr
(late 1950's)

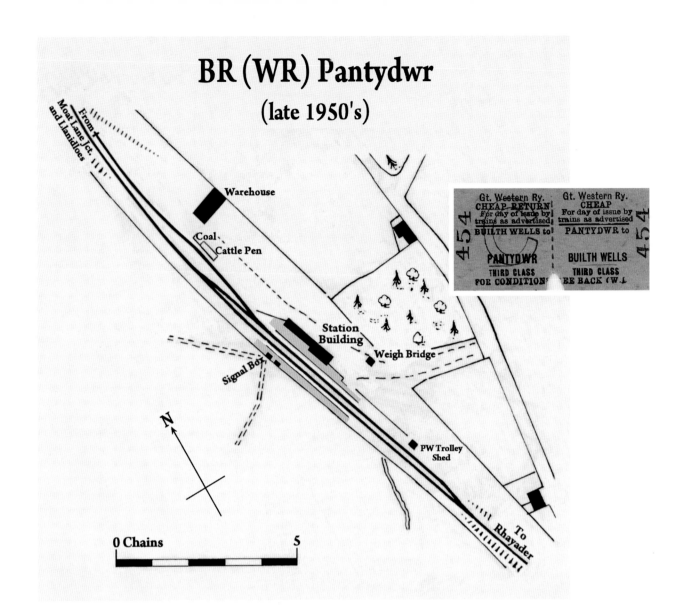

From Moat Lane Jct. and Llanidloes

Warehouse

Coal

Cattle Pen

Station Building

Signal Box

Weigh Bridge

N

PW Trolley Shed

To Rhayader

0 Chains   5

Gt. Western Ry.
CHEAP RETURN
For day of issue by
trains as advertised
BUILTH WELLS to
PANTYDWR
THIRD CLASS
FOR CONDITION

454

Gt. Western Ry.
CHEAP
For day of issue by
trains as advertised
PANTYDWR to
BUILTH WELLS
THIRD CLASS
EE BACK (W.)

454

(*left*) Pantydwr station was not only the highest point on the Mid Wales Line, but was the highest point on the entire Cambrian system at 947 feet. Having two platforms and a small yard to the north it was a rest and be thankful spot for engine crews approaching from either direction! The climb from Llanidloes was pretty relentless with only a primary stop at Tylwch and a 'hindrance' stop at Glan-yr-Afon for the driver! Gradients of 1 in 60, 75, 77, and 85 would be encountered. The southerly approach was not much better. The line would have been climbing virtually all the way from Three Cocks Junction (some 35 miles away!), interspersed with admittedly several stops and some downhill sections, but the section from Rhayader to Pantydwr had a fearsome seven miles of stiff gradients including sections of 1 in 60 and several at 1 in 75! **Photograph**: D. J. Lowe Collection

(*Right*) Dean Goods No.2484 is seen in Pantydwr with a train from Moat Lane, whilst a train from Brecon enters the up loop on 9th September 1949.
Photograph: The late H.C.Casserley/ R.M Casserley

(*Centre*) Thirteen years later in May 1962, and just to the north of the station, passenger trains repeat the same sequence, except this time the motive power on each train has been replaced by 'Mickey Mouse' Class 2 2-6-0 locomotives. Two sidings used to be here but by the time of this picture only one existed.
Photograph: The late N. Jones
D. J. Lowe Archive

(*Below*) Pantydwr was opened on 30th November 1891, the signal box (with a 13-lever frame) was on the up platform with a brick built shelter next to it. A PW Motor Trolley hut can just be seen on the left of picture.
Photograph: D. J. Lowe Archive

(*Above*) No.46513 brings a handful of wagons northwards through Pantydwr on the 10th August 1962. Although probably based at Moat Lane or Llanidloes at this time, the shed staff have initiated the new shed coding (89D) to the locomotive at the beginning of 1961, when Oswestry MPD changed from 89A to 89D. Note the relatively compact nature of the station site and that the need for watering facilities wasn't thought an issue here as it was mid way between Llanidloes and Rhayader

Photograph: P. Fisher Collection

(*Above*) About half a mile south of Pantydwr we have now picked up the Afon Marteg which can be seen on the right. In the far distance the line curves to the right where we will soon call by St Harmons. Note the bleak nature of the surroundings now.
Photograph: The late N. Jones/D. J. Lowe Archive

(*Above*) We arrive in St Harmons station and this view, looking north east, with the crossing gates open reveals the small siding that was present here. It was initially used for lime traffic and then general goods until the line was closed.
Photograph: D. J. Lowe Collection

(*Above*) The small community was named St Harmon, its name being taken from the traditional local church, but the railways added the 's' to its title. The station therefore first appeared in timetables in June 1872 as St Harmons. The 1892 signal box contained nine levers, but all staffing was withdrawn in 1936 except for a gatekeeper who was retained until closure. Just how many folks living in this part of Wales now would envy such a facility on their doorstep? **Photograph**: The late J. Fozard/S. Fozard

(*Above*) Departing from St Harmons and heading southwards, we cross over the Afon Marteg at the sixty eight and half miles marker post (from Whitchurch). The locomotive is No.46516 and was pulling the 9.55am ex. Moat Lane passenger for Brecon. Arrival time was sheduled for 12.35pm. The terrain continues to show a lack of trees with most areas given over to sheep pasturing.
Photograph: The late N. Jones/D. J. Lowe Archive

(*Right*) The returning ex Brecon 1.20pm train heading northwards just south west of St Harmons. Our train will have encountered some stiff gradients from Rhayader to this point including those of 1 in 90, 1 in 80 and 1 in 75 over a three to four mile stretch. This short section into St Harmons had a falling gradient of 1 in 530 and level before the climb continued to Pantydwr summit.
Photograph: The late N. Jones
                    D. J. Lowe Archive

(*Above*) Pictures of engineers trolleys parked up in the open like this one are few and far between. PW staff would carry a 'Section' key to unlock the trolley and give special access to a section of the line subject to the signalman controlling that section. This was pictured by Norman Jones as he returned to Moat Lane having footplated the line in both directions that day. We are about a quarter of a mile further west of our previous picture, in a very rural area where most of the lanes provided access only to remote country farms. In close proximity to the Afon Marteg, many lanes had fords running across them. 4th May 1962.

Photograph: The late N. Jones/D. J. Lowe Archive

GILFACH

(*Right*) At virtually the same spot as the previous picture but now looking southwest towards Marteg and Rhayader. The Afon Marteg winds its way down the valley amoungst the trees where the small locality of Gilfach, hidden by those trees in the middle of the picture, is sited. The mountainous terrain beckons beyond.
Photograph: The late N. Jones/D. J. Lowe Archive

(*Left*) At Gilfach, a brick lined tunnel, more commonly known as Marteg Tunnel, was the only option to the early builders of the line. This effectively took the railway through an outcrop of rock which the Afon Marteg went around. The railway crossed the river twice before entering the northern portal shown here.
Photograph: The late N. Jones/D. J. Lowe Archive

MARTEG
TUNNEL

(*Right*) The southern portal of the tunnel as an engine crew would have seen it as they headed northwards. A small track crossed over the outcrop above both portals providing an ideal location for photography as we shall see later! **Photograph**: The late N. Jones/D. J. Lowe Archive

(Above) Above Marteg Tunnel north portal looking at the lines approach. The tree (centre) obscures the first bridge over the Afon Marteg. The second bridge with an adjacent PW hut is lower right. Note that the Afon Marteg makes a complete 'U' turn at this point. It is very apparent in this view that the tunnel option was the only answer for the line builders. The line simply couldn't twist and turn as much as the river could at this point. Farmers have made the best of the valley flatlands with some forestry being undertaken on the slopes of some of the hills here

Photograph: D. J. Lowe Collection

(*Above*) I am indebted to the late Michael Hale for letting me use this picture. I first observed it in his "Steam in Mid Wales" book, published in 2004 and mentioned to him my long term project of doing a book on the Mid Wales Line someday. He was agreeable to helping me and it is with great sadness he is no longer with us to see his picture being used in this book. Taken from above the south portal at Marteg Tunnel, an ex LMS designed class 2 2-6-0 approaches the 372yd tunnel with the 1.20pm Brecon to Moat Lane Junction service.   **Photograph**: The late Michael Hale

MARTEG HALT

(*Left*) A train for Brecon passes the deminutive halt at Marteg on the 21st June 1962. A GWR initiative to cater for walkers and ramblers it was opened on 18th May 1931.
Photograph: Ben Ashworth

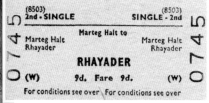

(*Below*) A waiting passenger at Marteg Halt makes use of the ex 1.20pm Brecon to Moat Lane service on 4th May 1962. The halt had a sleeper built platform and a corrugated waiting shelter, which looked to have been recently painted. Access from the adjacent main A44 road above was via a series of wooden steps. Note the Forestry warning sign depicting a black fir tree on a yellow background at the far end of the platform. This warned the driver he was about to enter an area with a high fire risk and to go steady with the regulator!
Photograph: The late N. Jones/D. J. Lowe Archive

BR (WR) Rhayader
(late 1950's)

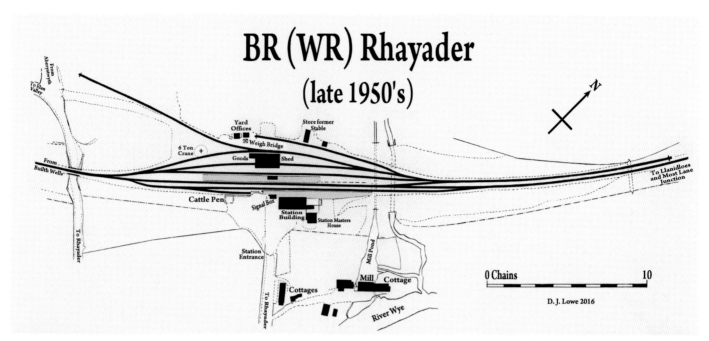

To Elan Valley
From Aberystwyth
From Builth Wells
To Rhayader
Yard Offices
Weigh Bridge
6 Ton Crane
Store former Stable
Goods Shed
Cattle Pen
Signal Box
Station Building
Station Masters House
Station Entrance
To Rhayader
Mill Pond
Cottages
Mill
Cottage
River Wye
To Llanidloes and Moat Lane Junction

N

0 Chains   10

D. J. Lowe 2016

(*Above*) There was a slight rising gradient of 1 in 690 into Rhayader station, (which was 21½ miles from Moat Lane). It was situated in the village of Llansantffraed-Cwmdeuddwr on the west bank of the River Wye and overlooked the town of Rhayader. Opened on 21st September 1864, the stone built station buildings and the signal box were on the down platform. This footplate view clearly shows the goods yard laid out with a series of loop sidings along with the stone built goods warehouse. The yard offices and another siding are hidden by the covered vans.
Photograph: The late N. Jones/D. J. Lowe Archive

(*Above*) General view of the station. The signal box was of 1891 vintage and had 19 levers. Note the rodding tunnel under the dock on the right, this was unusual. The water tank was half way down the 'down' platform and supplied the original MWR water columns. Beneath each of the running in boards proclaimed "For the Elan Valley Lakes". **Photograph**: R.G.Nelson/P. Fisher Collection. (*Centre*) Dean Goods No.2556 pauses with a southbound train in October 1951. **Photograph**: P. Fisher Collection. (*Below*) No. 46518 and two coaches wait alongside a PW trolley in the 'up' platform in 1961. **Photograph**: P. Fisher Collection.

(8503) 2nd PRIVILEGE RETURN	(8503) PRIVILEGE.2nd RETURN
Rhayader	Glan-yrAfonHalt
to	to
GLAN-YR-AFON HALT	RHAYADER
W) Fare 11½d.	Fare 11½d. (W)
For conditions see over	For conditions see over

Construction of the Dams and Reservoirs of the Elan Valley

(*Right*) The last of the Elan Valley dams to be constructed, the Claerwen dam and finished in 1952, culminated in sixty years of heavy civil engineering in the Elan Valley. From the early 1890's, Birmingham Corporations need for more water culminated in the system of reservoirs and dams in the Elan valley as we know them today. The Cambrian provided the south western end of its goods yard at Rhayader as a materials storage site for much of the constructions in the early days. Materials were transferred to an interchange yard called Noyadd Sidings, accessed from the specially built Elan Valley Junction (completed 1894) that was immediately to the south of Rhayader Tunnel pictured below.

The Birmingham Water Works Corporation (BWWC) operated their own railway service to the dams for construction purposes, although the Cambrian had offered this facility initially. The population swelled considerably during the construction period with many workers living in Elan Village or Llanidloes, and obviously much use of the Mid Wales Line to ferry workers about was required. The resulting dams and reservoirs became a major attraction and much of it was made by the railway authorities in providing horse buses from Rhayader for day out visits to this new engineering wonder. **Photograph**: D. J. Lowe Archive

(*left*) Just south of Rhayader station was Rhayader Tunnel and in this view we can see directly through the structure. Elan Valley Junction beyond the southern portal was eventually removed sometime around 1917, after the waterworks branch had slowly become foreshortened and eventually dismantled.
Photograph: The late N. Jones/D. J. Lowe Archive

(*Left*) Just over a mile south of Rhayader Tunnel, Cerrig Gwynion Quarry siding was passed, which became redundant in June 1956. However quarry blasting was still carried out on site, neccesitating permissions to be communicated between the Rhayader Station Master and the quarry company for the safe passage of trains. Shortly afterwards and running southwards, approximately half a mile north of Doldowlod, we have the River Wye accompanying the railway.

Photograph: The late N. Jones/D. J. Lowe Archive

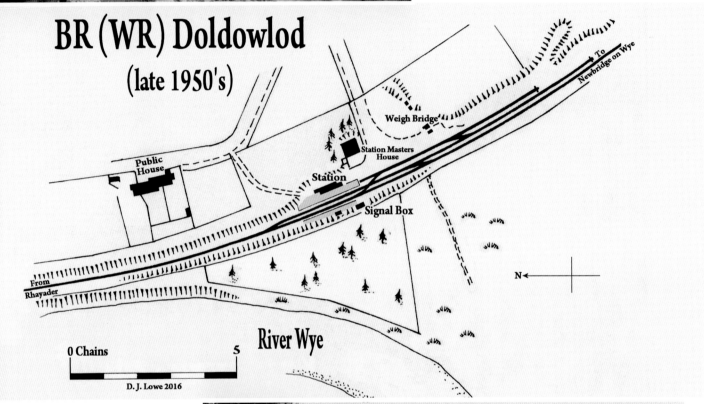

(*Right*) Doldowlod station (taking its name from a house two miles distant) was of timber construction with a slate tiled roof. It was situated on the down platform with access from the main road via a pathway. The signal box, opened 1891 contained an 18-lever frame and was sited on the 'up' platform along with a small shelter. The goods yard was to the south of the station and remained open until closure of the line. The signal box and the 'up' platform along with its running line were closed from June of 1962. The yard would sometimes stable a locomotive for banking purposes northwards where gradients as steep as 1 in 60 would be encountered before Pantydwr was reached.

Photograph: The late J. Fozard/S. Fozard

BR (WR) Newbridge-on-Wye
(late 1950's)

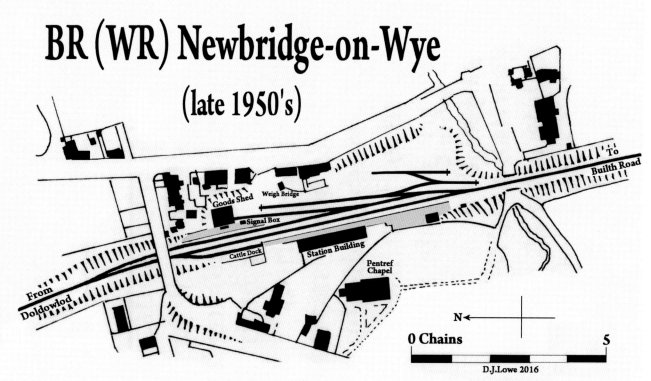

Goods Shed

Weigh Bridge

Signal Box

Cattle Dock

Station Building

Pentref Chapel

To Builth Road

From Doldowlod

N

0 Chains   5

D.J.Lowe 2016

(*Above*) This is Newbridge-on-Wye station looking northwards. Of brick contruction it was sited on the longer 'up' platform adjacent to a cattle dock. The shorter 'down' platform played host to the signal box and the brick built waiting shelter. A large wooden goods warehouse was to the rear of the shorter platform, the yard contained two main sidings and two private sidings formerly used by two timber handling companies, namely Thomas and Watts. These had additional single sidings (up until their removal in 1938) respectively south and north of the station.
Photograph: G. J. Biddle

(*Above*) Ivatt class 2 2-6-0 No.46518 brings its two coaches into Newbridge-on-Wye with a service from Moat Lane Junction. The locomotive is one of those in the class in the BR green lined out livery. Several Mid Wales Line class 2 engines had this livery applied when they visited Swindon for major overhauls from 1957 onwards, but modellers beware, some still came out in the lined out black MT livery! The coaches behind are of Hawksworth and Collett vintage in maroon and blood and custard. June 1958.
Photograph: The late Colin Caddy Collection

(*Centre*) A general view from the bridge showing the cattle dock in the right foreground. Note the concrete washing down apron around the track. The signal box of typical style for the line was built in 1891 and contained 14-levers. The yard handled goods traffic right up to closure.
Photograph: P. Fisher Collection

(*Left*) A view of Class 2 No.46516 about to set off for Brecon on 4th May 1962. The reader will appreciate the well maintained infrastructure characteristic of the line. Just seven months before complete closure.
Photograph: The late N. Jones
D. J. Lowe Archive

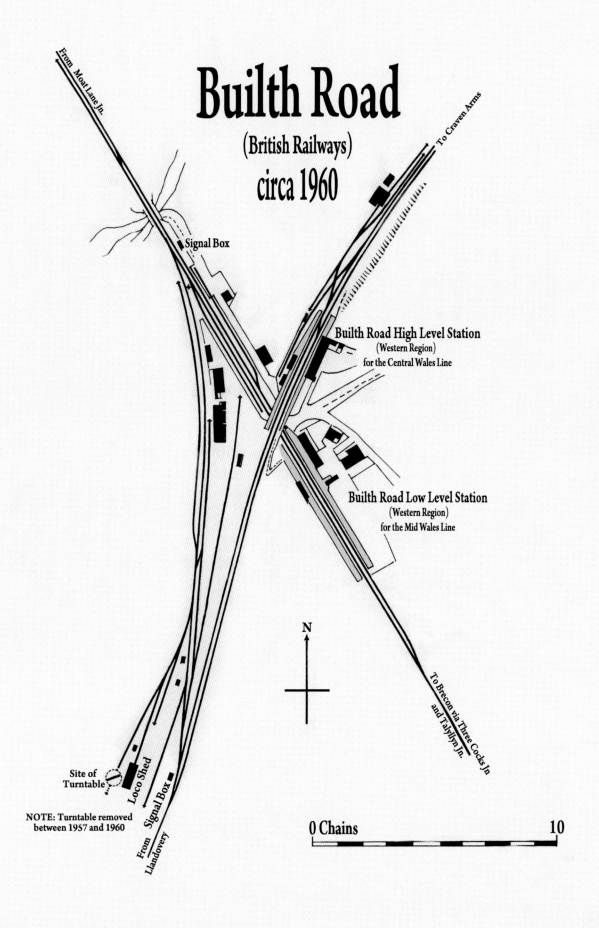

Builth Road

(British Railways)

circa 1960

From Moat Lane Jn.

To Craven Arms

Signal Box

Builth Road High Level Station
(Western Region)
for the Central Wales Line

Builth Road Low Level Station
(Western Region)
for the Mid Wales Line

N

To Brecon via Three Cocks Jn
and Talyllyn Jn.

Site of
Turntable

Loco Shed

From Signal Box
Llandovery

NOTE: Turntable removed
between 1957 and 1960

0 Chains   10

(*Above*) Builth Road Low Level station buildings were sited on the 'down' platform and were of rendered stone and included a refreshment room. The 'up' platform had a brick built shelter. Having intially two signal boxes, the south box was dispensed with in 1935, whereas the north box became Builth Road Low Level from 1935 and can be seen under the bridge. A ramp and pathway connected the station with Builth Road High Level station and a baggage tower was provided for easing transshipment between the two stations. No 46511 arrives with a train for Brecon on 24th August 1962. **Photograph**: Ben Ashworth

(*Above*) Running into Builth Road LL heading southwards, the landmark luggage tower can be seen sticking above the bridge parapet. The Central Wales Line crosses over the Mid Wales Line at this point.The engineers depot is on the extreme right with a load of coal mineral wagons in the loop refuge siding right centre.**Photograph**: The late N. Jones/D. J. Lowe Archive

(*Above*) Originally named Lechryd, Builth Road was adopted from May 1889 with a further revision to Builth Road Low Level on 1st January 1950. In this superb view by Ben Ashworth, he has managed to capture just about everything thats going! Ex LMS class 8F No.48354 arrives in the High Level station with a South Wales to Shrewsbury passenger train, meanwhile Class 2 No.46516 gets the starting signal for its train to Moat Lane in the Low Level on 29th August 1962. **Photograph**: Ben Ashworth

(*Above*) The running in board on the 'down' platform indicating to passengers should they need to change for stations on the Central Wales route. 1959.
Photograph: D. J. Lowe Collection

(*Left*) Its strange how nick names stuck with certain classes of locomotive. The 'Mickey Mouse' label associated with the LMS designed Ivatt class 2 2-6-0 perhaps was a most endearing one and No.46516, in the black mixed traffic livery, personifies it typically. In charge of two Hawksworth coaches it will be departing shortly with the ex.1.20pm Brecon train for Moat Lane Junction on 24th August 1962.
Photograph: Ben Ashworth

(*Above*) A quick visit to Builth Road High Level (a former ex LNWR station) and we catch ex LMS 8F No.48706 taking on water at the column prior to departing for South Wales with a mixed freight train. The locomotice was an 87F Llanelly engine at the time and a regular performer on the Central Wales line. Picture was taken from the bridge directly over the Mid Wales line. Early 1960's.
Photograph: D. J. Lowe Archive

(*Above*) A view of BR Standard class 5 4-6-0 No.73090 setting off from the High Level with a train for South Wales on 4th June 1964. At this time the Mid Wales line had closed, but the ex.LNWR engineers yard and exchange sidings on the right were still in existence. Left of signal in the distance can be seen the signal box controlling the yard and cord, and to the right the disused former engine shed.
Photograph: Ben Ashworth

(*Right*) No. 46508 makes use of the yard facilities on 29th August 1962. The turntable here was 'recovered' sometime between 1956 and 1960. Although a cord connected the Mid Wales and the Central Wales lines any through train services are sketchy although certain 'Spa' trains are perported to have run up until 1939.
Photograph: Ben Ashworth

BUILTH ROAD ENGINE SHED

(*Left*) No.46523 on shed at Builth Road (84G later 89A) on 12th April 1959. **Photograph**: D. J. Lowe Archive

(*Below*) The 12.10pm Swansea to Shrewsbury train enters the High Level station while on the right the cord can be seen passing through part of the exchange and engineers yard. Note the stacked trackwork behind the crane from part of the dismantled Mid Wales line. A June 1964 view.
Photograph: Ben Ashworth

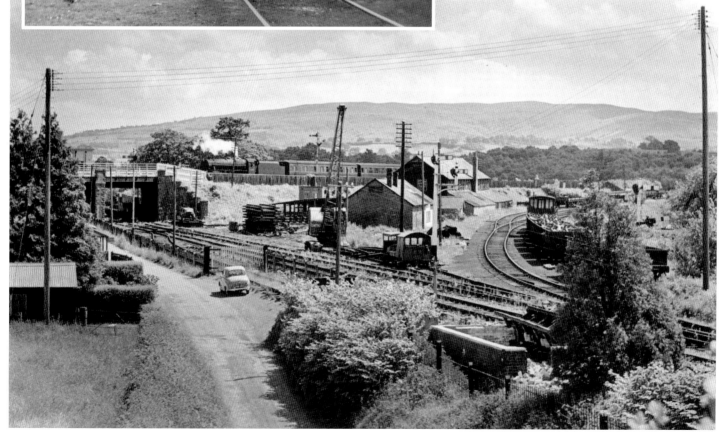

(*Above*) Beauty of the Mid Wales Line. One mile south east of Builth Road, Ben Ashworth found this lovely location besides the fast flowing River Wye. No.46505 scurries by with the 2.35pm ex.Newtown to Brecon train on 25th August 1962. The A479 main road (now A470), runs immediately above the train.

Photograph: Ben Ashworth

BR (WR) Builth Wells
(circa 1960)

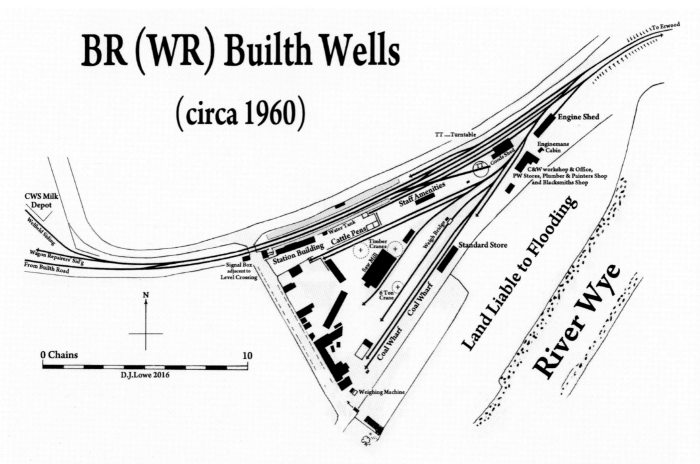

To Erwood

Engine Shed

TT ....Turntable

Enginemans Cabin

Goods Shed

C&W workshop & Office, PW Stores, Plumber & Painters Shop and Blacksmiths Shop

CWS Milk Depot

Wellfield Siding

Wagon Repairers' Sid'g

From Builth Road

Signal Box adjacent to Level Crossing

Station Building

Cattle Pens

Water Tank

Staff Amenities

Timber Cranes

Saw Mill

6 Ton Crane

Weigh Bridge

Standard Store

Coal Wharf

Coal Wharf

Land Liable to Flooding

River Wye

Weighing Machine

N

0 Chains   10

D.J.Lowe 2016

(*Above*) Ivatt class 2 No.46515 on 'up' mixed goods duties is halted in the station at Builth Wells on 29th August 1962. There appears to be a lot of coal being transported, possibly for the local gas works or loco depots further up the line, along with a covered van and a conflat container. The main A479 road crossed here adjacent to the main station buildings. **Photograph**: Ben Ashworth

BUILTH WELLS

(*Above*) The station was of stone block construction with adjoining station house sited on the 'up' platform. The water tank was a post war improvement to provide a better supply from one previously located next to the station house. The 'down' platform boasted a brick built waiting shelter and gents toilets. **Photograph**: G. J. Biddle

(*Above*) Looking eastwards towards Brecon in the 'down' direction the goods warehouse can be seen behind the stored coaches with the yard to the right. A single road engine shed existed up until September 1957. Originally two signal boxes, North and South were on the 'down side but replaced in 1932 with one sited on the 'up' side by the level crossing. **Photograph**: D. J. Lowe Archive

(*Above*) An engine is preparing two coaches for the 12.30pm return to Brecon whilst in the background can be seen Llanelwedd quarry. The turntable near the goods shed is just obscured by the end of platform fence, whilst the yard had small workshop facilities for locomotive, signalling and permanent way departments. A 1958 view. **Photograph**: P. Fisher Collection.

(*Left*) View of the station house with main station building beyond. The old water tank used to be sited extreme right above building. The covered van is standing at the end of the cattle pens siding. **Photograph**: D. J. Lowe Archive

(*Above*) The 1932 GWR replacement signal box for Builth Wells was sited by the level crossing and was a typical wooden type favoured by the company.
Photograph: D. J. Lowe Archive

(*Above*) The Builth Wells goods warehouse showing the locoshed (right) which was closed in September 1957. Note the filled in Turntable pit in the left foreground (recovered December 1961).
Photograph: P. Fisher Collection.

Gt. Western Ry. | Gt. Western Ry.
CHEAP RETURN | CHEAP
For day of issue by | For day of issue by
trains as advertised | trains as advertised
BUILTH WELLS to | PANTYDWR to
454 | 454
PANTYDWR | BUILTH WELLS
THIRD CLASS | THIRD CLASS
FOR CONDITION | EE BACK (W.I

Gt Western Ry - Gt Western Ry
H.M. FORCES ON LEAVE
Builth Wells | Builth Wells
992 | 992
TO
BRECON
THIRD CLASS
Brecon | Brecon
FOR CONDITIONS SEE BACK A.I

(*Above*) Running into Builth Wells for Brecon, we see the PW staff digging out to reballast some of the trackwork in the platform road. The Mid Wales line was maintained to the highest level right up until closure, which made it an even more bitter pill to swallow when the end came. May 1962.
Photograph: The late N. Jones/D. J. Lowe Archive

(*Above*) Most trains, in either direction would stop at Builth Wells for water. Here the crew are replenishing the tender of No.46516 as it makes its way with the ex.9.55am from Moat Lane on 4th May 1962. On departure, within the next half mile it would pass Llanelwedd quarry sidings.
Photograph: The late N. Jones/D. J. Lowe Archive

(*Above left*) A 1935 view of the Loco shed at Builth Wells showing its brick supporting lower wall with upper corrugated panels and roof. Two 0-6-0 tender locomotives were usually allocated here. In 1947 Nos 895 and 2556 were the resident engines. On 20th July 1952, Nos 2343, 2538 and 5801 were present! When British Railways introduced the oval shed codes in 1950, Builth Wells shared the code 89B as a sub shed with its larger near neighbour Brecon shed. In the early post war years some modification to the roof had been carried out (*right picture*) with it remaining in use up until 14th September 1957. This picture shows it still extant in April 1959. The turntable was removed from here in December 1961.

Photographs: The late H.C.Casserley/R.M Casserley and D. J. Lowe Archive

(*Above*) No.46505 is on one of those typical mid line shuttles starting at Builth Road at 12.30 pm and arriving at Brecon at 2.27pm. The engine with its two coaches is seen in Builth Wells having arrived here at 12.33pm.There will be a prolonged wait here before departing for Brecon at 1.15pm. June 1959.

Photograph: Ben Ashworth

(*Above*) As the reader will be aware, not all of the service trains ran from one end of the line to the other. There were several shuttle services between some of the principle stations on the line. Here John Langford has managed to catch two such services in one go. Taken from the 9.10am Builth Road LL to Three Cocks Junction passenger train, (this service getting into the latter station at 10.04am), we observe the ex.8.15am Brecon to Builth Road LL train, hauled by No.46518, setting back into the siding to detach two rear coaches before it continues to Builth Road LL, arriving at 9.44am. Note the block and tie rod method of track construction in the siding on the left. The River Wye keeps company with the railway in close proximity at this point. The date is 14th April 1962

Photograph: John Langford.

(*Above*) A northbound train makes its way into Builth Wells. The town's wells were noted for their saline and sulphur content and as with the Spa's at neighbouring Llanwrtyd Wells, Llangammarch Wells, and Llandrindod Wells, were extremely popular in the early days and brought many tourists to the area. The station at Builth Wells was effectively in the village of Llanelwedd (in Radnorshire) across the river from the actual town (in Breconshire). Much of the station layout can be seen in this picture including the station buildings, goods warehouse, yard and engine shed.

Photograph: Ben Ashworth

(*Above*) Just before 3.00pm on a glorious summers afternoon, the ex.10.15am 'down' freight from Moat Lane Junction has made it as far as Llanfaredd Halt, which it is just passing. The train consists of a number of mineral wagons, some containing stone from the quarry at Llanelwedd and some 'empties' which probably contained coal on their earlier northerly trip. In addition there are two break vans and a covered van. After several other stops en route it will eventually arrive at Brecon Yard at 8.15pm!

Photograph: Ben Ashworth

(*Above*) Llanfaredd Halt c 1950's. Another halt put in by the GWR, opening on 7th May 1934 to attract walkers and the tourist market. As one would expect only the basic facilities were provided. **Photograph**: The late H.C.Casserley/R.M Casserley

(*Above*) Aberedw was a simple brick shelter with two sidings just to the south of the platform, (facing from the direction of Erwood) and worked from a ground frame locked by the electric token. They were worked by 'down' trains only and could only be accessed when Erwood Signal box was switched into circuit.The line was on a gradient of 1 in 112 falling to Builth Wells. Looking in 'up' direction on 20th August 1961. **Photograph**: D. J. Lowe Archive

(*Above*) A delightful view across the River Wye showing No.46520 running southwards on the 12.30pm Builth Road to Brecon service on 25th August 1962. The train will have just passed the private single platform at milepost 92 of Tyr-Celyn halt. This short platform did not appear in the public timetable and was for the residents of a nearby private house. It was in use from 1872 until 1950. The B4567 road is by the waters edge!

Photograph: Ben Ashworth

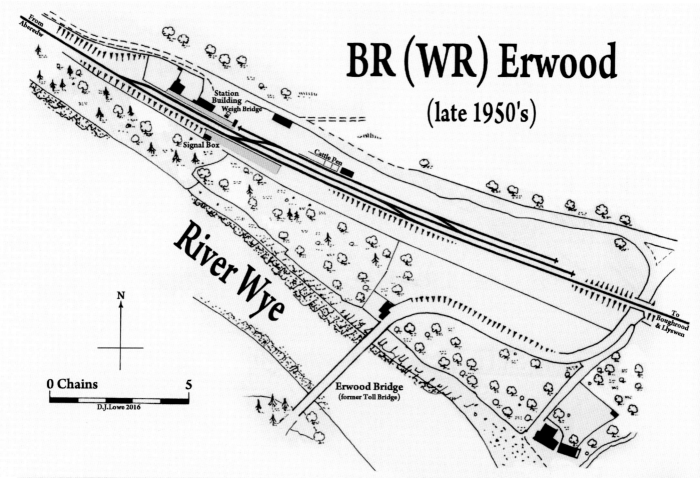

BR (WR) Erwood
(late 1950's)

From Abaredw

Station Building

Weigh Bridge

Signal Box

Cattle Pen

River Wye

N

0 Chains 5

D.J.Lowe 2016

Erwood Bridge
(former Toll Bridge)

To Boughrood & Llyswen

(*Above*) The picturesque Erwood station was perhaps the most photogenic on the line. In this May 1959 picture we can see a goods train departing for Builth Wells. Of note are the staggered platforms, and the passenger walkway from the end of the 'up' platform to the middle of the 'down' one requiring a big step up!

Photograph: G. J. Biddle

(*Above*) A wonderful view of Erwood taken by John Fozard in the early 1960's. The timber built station building with tiled roof has an original MWR passenger seat infront with the latest railway posters afixed behind for prospective holiday makers to view. The corrugated store/lamp room is perched on the end of the 'down' platform with the goods yard behind including the 'dock' and goods warehouse. The yard closed when passenger services were withdrawn. The station building until recently was still extant as a craft and souvenir shop.

Photograph: The late J. Fozard/S. Fozard

(*Above*) Looking at the 'up' platform the signal box of 1891 contained an 18-lever frame. A brick built waiting shelter can be seen to the left. The passenger walkway is visible in the right foreground.   Photograph: D. J. Lowe Archive

(*Right*)   H.C.Casserley   witnessed ex.CamR. 0-6-0 No.887 on goods duties as he waited on his northbound train in Erwood station on 9th September 1949. There was a railway bungalow on the 'down' platform which can be seen on the left of picture. The actual village of Erwood was about three quarters of a mile away on the other side of the River Wye, but the siting of the station required it to be built where it was because of the railways track keeping to the north eastern side of the river.

Photograph:The late H.C.Casserley
              R.M Casserley

(*Above*) One mile to the south east of Erwood the line has to cross the Bach Howey, a small tributary of the River Wye. The railway crosses it by this bridge, originally designated as 'Bridge R' by the MWR. To the right one can see where the stream flows into the Wye. No.46516 is heading northwards with the 1.20pm Brecon to Moat Lane passenger train on 28th August 1962. **Photograph**: Ben Ashworth

Note how the old triangular bridge suport has been infilled with concrete to give greater supporting strength to the bridge spans

(*Above*) Continuing southwards, the railway has been slowly channelled into the ever narrowing Wye valley with steeper hillsides. Two miles south of Erwood we run into Llanstephan Radnor Halt. Another GWR creation for the tourist market, it was opened on 6th March 1933. Access was from a step cinder path down from near the road over bridge. This early 1960's view shows once again the well maintained look of the place, with the corrugated waiting shelter looking as though it has recently received a lick of paint.   **Photograph**: The late J. Fozard/S. Fozard

(*Above*) No.46505 on the 12.30pm Builth Road to Brecon train makes a cautious approach at Llanstephan Radnor Halt on 28th August 1962. These former GWR halts were built mainly for the tourist market to encourage walkers to the area and were very basic. Note the sleeper constructed platform and the provision of a lamp holder next to the running in board. This would have a lit lamp provided by a guard from a later running train for the hours of darkness.Once spent, the lamp would be collected by another guard next morning for refilling and reuse later that day.

Photograph: Ben Ashworth

BR (WR) Boughrood
& Llyswen

(late 1950's)

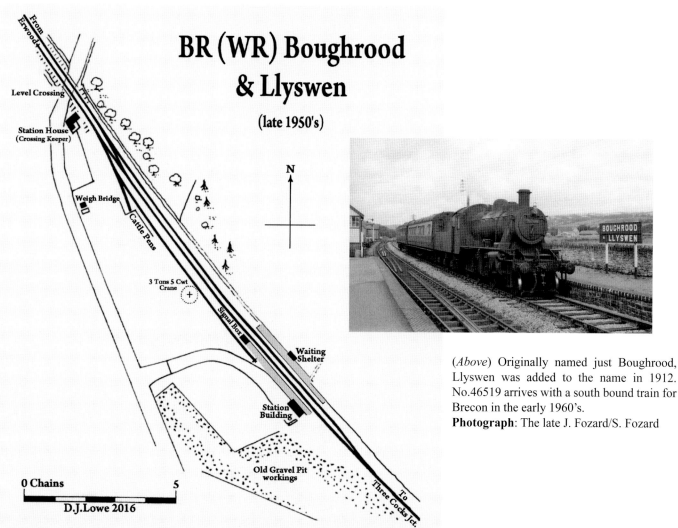

(Above) Originally named just Boughrood, Llyswen was added to the name in 1912. No.46519 arrives with a south bound train for Brecon in the early 1960's.

Photograph: The late J. Fozard/S. Fozard

(Above) Class 2 No.46518 waits patiently with a late afternoon train at Boughrood and Llyswen prior to departing for Brecon in June 1958. The station buildings and the signal box were on the 'up' platform and a gate keeper lived in a railway house by the crossing gates further up the line. The church steeple of Boughrood can be seen in the village on the right.

Photograph: The late Colin Caddy Collection

(*Above*) A general view of Boughrood and Llyswen station showing the timber constructed main station building. Several small store sheds feature on the 'up' platform. There was a timber built shelter on the 'down' platform which was the only provision for passengers. The crossing gates can clearly be seen in this view also the crossing keepers house. There was a small goods yard over to the left with cattle pens and a yard crane. The headshunt crossed the level crossing and ran parallel with the main running line for a short way.

Photograph: D. J. Lowe Collection.

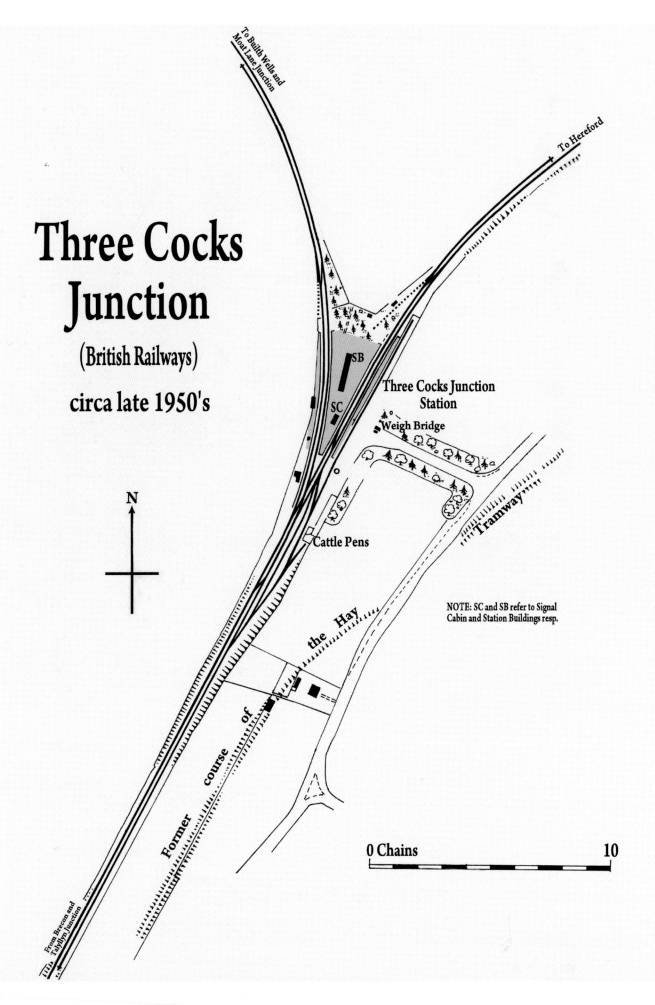

Three Cocks
Junction

(British Railways)

circa late 1950's

To Builth Wells and
Moat Lane Junction

To Hereford

SB

SC

Three Cocks Junction
Station

Weigh Bridge

Tramway

N

Cattle Pens

NOTE: SC and SB refer to Signal
Cabin and Station Buildings resp.

Former course of the Hay

From Brecon and
Talyllyn Junction

0 Chains   10

(*Above*) The view running into Three Cocks Junction from the Mid Wales Line. The River Wye departs company with the line near here and swings north eastwards towards Glasbury (about one mile to the north of the Junction). Our train has just crossed over the Afon Llynfi (a tributary of the Wye) which we shall now keep company with for the next few miles.
Photograph: The late N. Jones/D. J. Lowe Archive

(*Above*) The station buildings on the 'down' Mid Wales platform with the signal box. A refreshment room was provided at the station. The 'up' platform to the right of picture just had a brick waiting shelter. The view dates to 13th September 1956.   **Photograph**:The late H.C.Casserley/R.M Casserley

(*Above*) For large parts of the day, Three Cocks Junction would be quite a tranquil place. In the summer it could be sublime! All of a sudden the peace would be shattered as three trains would arrive in succession. In this view the 12.42pm train from Hereford, behind No.46522, has arrived on the right (at 1.47pm). Centre stage is the ex.12.30 pm train from Builth Road (having arrived at 1.48pm) for Brecon, behind No.46514, and on the left another Class 2 has brought in the ex.1.25pm Brecon to Moat Lane train. Notice the passengers off the Hereford train transferring to the Brecon train. This is so the Hereford train can run around its stock for its return to Hereford, to save unnessecary route mileage to Brecon. This scheme was introduced in the early 1950's as an economy measure. The date here is June 1959.

Photograph: D. J. Lowe Archive.

(*Above*) The signalman walks back to his signal box which was commissioned on 26th October 1890 replacing an older box almost opposite. The 'new' box contained 40-levers. The notice board on the gable wall of the building states that it is the Refreshment Room. (*Below*) A general view of the Hereford platforms with a basic shelter on the platform on the right. Notice the attractive tree screening and the Post Office van on the right. **Both Photographs**: The late N. Jones/D. J. Lowe Archive

(*Left*) Ex. Cambrian Jones goods No.896 is seen in the 'down' Mid Wales platform at Three Cocks Junction having sauntered down from Moat Lane with the 9.55am train on 11th September 1951. Also designated the '15' class they were originally judged to heavy for the Mid Wales Line but having this restriction waived during WWII some continued into the early 1950's until withdrawal came. The running in board on the 'up' platform advises passengers 'change for Hay & Hereford Line'.
Photograph: The late H.C.Casserley
R.M Casserley

(*Right*) Historically the Hereford line allowed the former Midland Railway (MR) and later London Midland and Scottish (LMS) access into southwest Wales via Brecon. This in turn resulted in lightweight locomotives of those earlier companies mixing with ex.Cambrian/GWR and early BR types. Here we see MR Johnson 3F 0-6-0 No.43600 on the ex.1.10pm Brecon to Hereford service in the platform at Three Cocks Junction on 9th September 1949.
Photograph: The late H.C.Casserley
R.M Casserley

(*Left*) Literally in the twilight of its life, the last running Dean Goods No.2538 is about to set off from Three Cocks Junction with the ex.5.05pm Brecon train to Moat Lane Junction. Taken on 13th September 1956 it would be nearly dark by the time the train reaches its destination. What a wonderful journey the passengers would have had travelling northwards that evening. No.2538 was supposedly confined to the Kerry branch at this date!
Photograph: R.M Casserley

(*Above*) All looks fine with the world in this view at Three Cocks Junction, but in seven days time, the railway would be closing. Its heartbreaking to dwell on how railwaymen and women must have been feeling at this time, still being required to maintain a public service right up to the very end. No.46526 takes centre stage,whilst the Hereford train looks to have come in on the station building platform side. 22nd December 1962. **Photograph**: Graham Jackson Collection

(*Above*) In lovely Spring light this 1961 view shows the Moat Lane to Brecon train leaving Three Cocks Junction behind Class 2 No.46505. Note in the station the Hereford train already to depart, with the engine facing tender first, while on the left the train for Moat Lane is also preparing to make a start. **Photograph**: D. J. Lowe Archive.

BR (WR) Talgarth
(late 1950's)

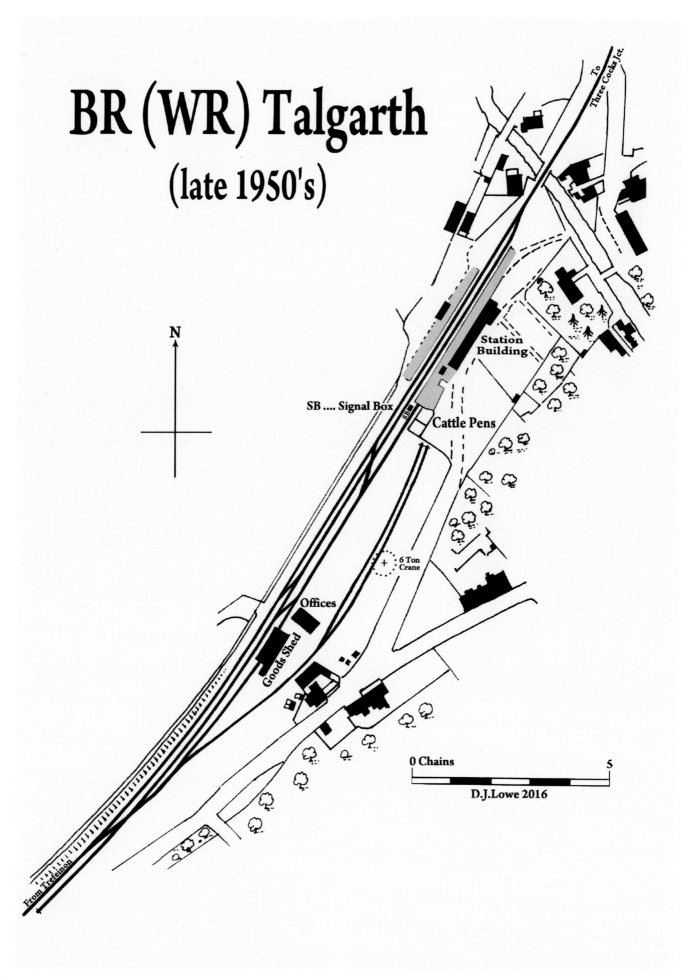

To Three Cocks Jct.

N

Station Building

SB .... Signal Box

Cattle Pens

6 Ton Crane

Offices

Goods Shed

From Trefeinon

0 Chains 5

D.J.Lowe 2016

(*Above and right*) The crew of Class 2 No.46516 have this view of Talgarth station on 4th May 1962. The substantial stone built station building stands on the 'down' platform adjacent to the water tank which may be seen just above the locomotives smokebox. There appears to be a few takers on the platform for the journey onwards to Brecon. The signal box can be seen a little further on. As common to most stations on the Mid Wales Line, accommodation for passengers on the 'up' platform is a little less generous, with the customary shelter but with fairly elaborate barge boards provided! It will be noticed that both the water columns on the platforms are the original MWR ones, and a close up of the one at the southern end of the 'down' platform is pictured on the right. A spacious goods yard was behind the signalbox as was a large warehouse which can just be seen left of centre.
Photograph: The late N. Jones/D. J. Lowe Archive

Gt. Western Ry Gt. Western Ry
Rhayader   Rhayader
TO
TALGARTH
THIRD CLASS
4/7 C Fare 4/7 C
Talgarth   Talgarth
FOR CONDITIONS SEE BACK WD

(*Top*) Looking northwards, the main station buildings including the water tank. **Photograph**: G. J. Biddle

(*Left centre*) The 'up' platform, showing the elaborate waiting shelter. The station still had two or three original MWR seats on the platforms. The Afon Llynfi flowed under the railway to the north of the platforms. **Photograph**: The late J. Fozard/S. Fozard

(*Right*) Talgarth Signal Box of 1891 vintage had an upgrade from 18 to 26 levers in 1956. The cattle dock was position to the rear of it. **Photograph**: P Fisher Collection

(*Above*) Talgarth goods yard lay to the south of the station. Over the years the layout had changed which might account for the signal box upgrade in 1956. The goods warehouse was effectively on a loop, which also accessed the cattle dock. In addition there were two long sidings with a 6-ton yard crane. The engine, No.46516 is obscuring the signal box on the left, but it was the signalmans respondsibility to ensure passengers crossed the lines safely by means of the crossing in the centre foreground. The usual warning signs and the setting down apparatus can be seen on the right. The date is 4th May 1962. **Photograph**: The late N. Jones/D. J. Lowe Archive

(*Above*) The last week of operation of the Mid Wales Line coincided with Great Britain being carpeted in a blanket of snow. It therefore was to be expected that this part of Wales would receive some significant falls. Not being daunted by this, John Fozard was able to record this wintry scene at Talgarth during that last week of operation. Once again we see No.46516 performing to the end, as it pauses briefly in the station before making its long wintry way northwards to Moat Lane. A demanding ordeal for the crew, one can only ponder and admire.

Photograph: The late J. Fozard/S. Fozard

(*Above*) Two and half miles to the southwest of Talgarth we reach the small station of Trefeinon. Originally this had just a single platform with a siding, but around 1907 this was coverted into a loop and a second platform built. A new siding running behind the station building was then added. In the early summer of 1961 No.46516 is running into the 'up' platform road, as by this time the station no longer utilised the 'down' running line, it being closed along with the signal box in the November of 1959. A gate keeper was retained to operate the crossing gates until the line closed

Photograph: The late J. Fozard/S. Fozard

(*Above*) A train departs Trefeinon for Brecon, in this June 1959 view when both running lines and the signal box, just visible by the crossing, were still used. Note the basic, but adequate structures provided. The building on the right mimics several buildings we have already come across at other stations enroute.   **Photograph**: G. J. Biddle

(*Above*) Looking out of the cab of No.46516 as we pass through Trefeinon and approach the level crossing, we can see the disused loop on our left. Note how the flowers have grown and cascaded over the point rodding! **Photograph**: The late N. Jones/D. J. Lowe Archive

(*Above*) One and three quarter miles onwards, the GWR perhaps had a greater justification for putting a platform at Llangorse Lake Halt to cater for the tourists of the 1930's. There was an easy walk to Llangorse Lake, the largest natural lake in South Wales. A corrugated shelter was all they were going to get though on the platform!   **Photograph**: The late J. Fozard/S. Fozard

(*Above*) Our train we have been travelling down to Brecon on makes a stop at Llangorse Lake Halt on 4th May 1962. We see the train's guard, with flag under his arm, observing who is getting off and those who are joining the train. Note the drivers restricted view of the coaches with them being on a slight curve of the line.   **Photograph**: The late N. Jones/D. J. Lowe Archive

(*Above*) We are approaching Talyllyn North Junction. The line to Talyllyn Junction West diverges right here whilst the line going off to the left is for Talyllyn Junction East. Although the latter line was worked as a single line there were parallel through sidings on either side of it; the siding on the down side (left) was called the 'Mid Wales Siding' while that right was called the 'Midland Siding', names past down the years from earlier times. Original MWR property extended approximately halfway down each of the North and East Curves. The rest of the junction was owned originally by the Brecon and Merthyr with running powers granted to the Mid Wales et al. Sidings were to the top side of the North Curve, and in earlier times to the right of our train in the picture. The course of the old Hay Railway once followed a similar route along the northside of the North curve.

Photograph: The late N. Jones/D. J. Lowe Archive

Talyllyn Junction as at 1960

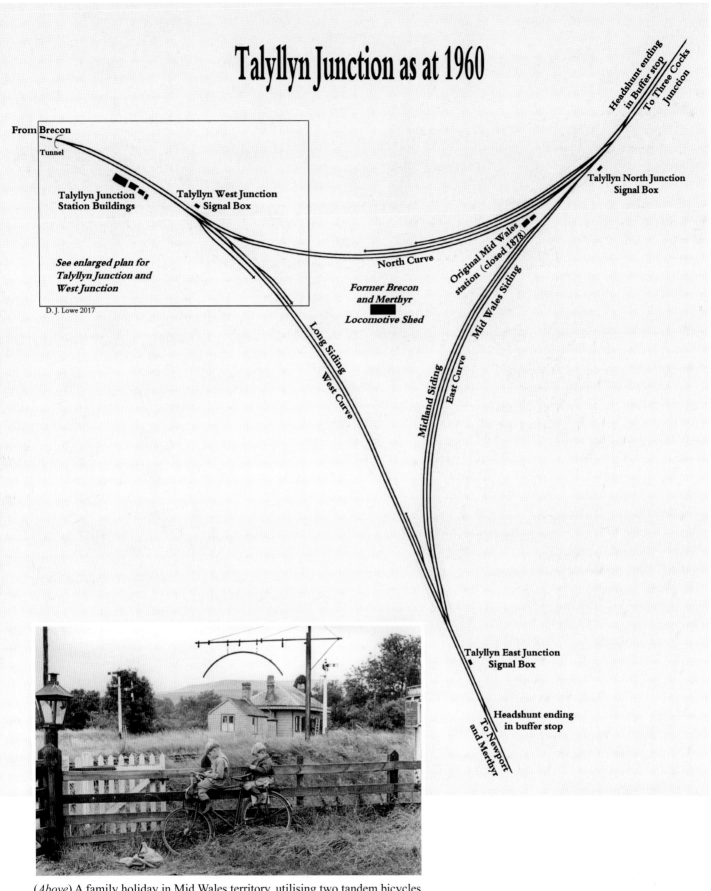

From Brecon

Tunnel

Talyllyn Junction
Station Buildings

Talyllyn West Junction
Signal Box

*See enlarged plan for
Talyllyn Junction and
West Junction*

D. J. Lowe 2017

North Curve

Former Brecon
and Merthyr
Locomotive Shed

Headshunt ending
in Buffer stop

To Three Cocks
Junction

Talyllyn North Junction
Signal Box

Original Mid Wales
station (closed 1878)

Mid Wales Siding

Long Siding

West Curve

Midland Siding

East Curve

Talyllyn East Junction
Signal Box

Headshunt ending
in buffer stop

To Newport
and Merthyr

(*Above*) A family holiday in Mid Wales territory, utilising two tandem bicycles,
presented Ben Ashworth with this opportunity of photographing his two sons
infront of the original MWR station buildings at Talyllyn North junction! These
were still extant in August 1962.   **Photograph**: Ben Ashworth

BR (WR) Talyllyn Junction
and Talyllyn West Junction
(Circa 1960)

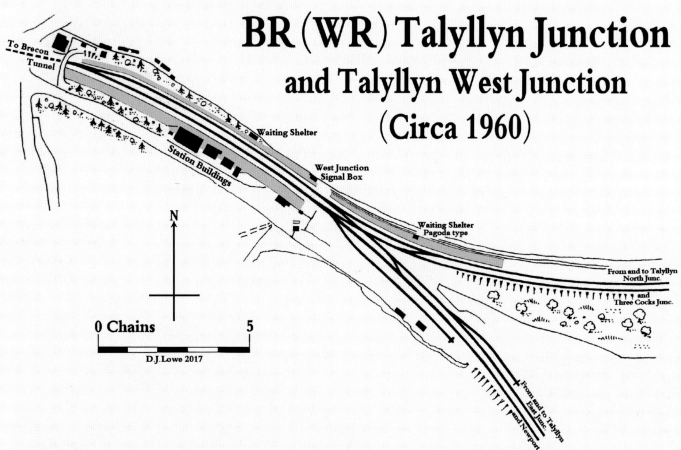

(*Above*) Class 2 No.46509 gets the all clear to run over the West Junction and into Talyllyn Junction station with a train off the Mid Wales Line sometime in 1961. In this picture we can see the "Extension Platform" which was added to Talyllyn Junction Station in 1895 to improve connections and to prevent congestion in the station environs. It was privilaged to have a GWR Pagoda shed for its shelter! Lines to Newport and Merthyr head of behind the locomotive and past the siding and dock on the right. The finger board signs to aid passengers in the left foreground were recently auctioned at a railwayana sale! **Photograph**: D. J. Lowe Archive

(*Above*) No.46503 poses with its 'up' train by Talyllyn Junction West Signal Box on 21st October 1955. The locomotive is in plain black livery and the early BR lion on wheel emblem can be seen on the tender. The coaching stock appears to be fairly clean in the Blood and Custard livery and the train would have looked very smart winding its way up to Moat Lane. A train from Newport stands at the platform on the left. The signal box was a substantial building with a stone built base and sited at the end of the ex.B&M's 'down' platform by the passenger walkway.

Photograph: D. J. Lowe Archive

(*Above*) No.46516 stands waiting to depart Talyllyn Junction station. We can see the extension platform with the passenger walkway just infront of the engine. Great care was demanded when members of the public were crossing the lines especially if a train from Newport or Merthyr was also in the station area. **Photograph**: Ben Ashworth

(*Above*) A general view of the station at Talyllyn Junction in June 1959. Note that we are now in ex.B&M territory, so that in earlier days the MWR would have negotiated running powers over this section to Brecon. Trains travelling from Talyllyn East Junction to Brecon were classed as 'up' trains, so 'down' trains from the Mid Wales Line via the North Curve became 'up' trains when running into Talyllyn Junction station. The main stone built station buildings, included a refreshment room and a public bar, and were situated on the ex.B&M's 'up' platform (left platform here). A substantial stone and brick edged shelter was on the opposite platform which complemented the style of the signal box, adjacent to which stood an elegant bracket signal guarding the West Junction. No.46522 was in charge of the 1.25pm ex.Brecon to Moat Lane 3-coach train and would be away at 1.40pm shortly. **Photograph**: D. J. Lowe Archive

(*Above*) The 9.55am ex.Moat Lane Junction train hauled by 46516, stands in the station at Talyllyn on the 4th May 1962. it will depart for Brecon at 12.25pm, five minutes before the train in the adjacent platform, the 12.10pm train from Brecon to Newport.
Photograph: D. J. Lowe Archive

(*Above*) Taken a month earlier to the picture above, John Langford was able to record this view of the same trains passing in the station. The Pannier tank is No.4611 which was based at 86A Ebbw Junction shed for several years. The usual 'Mickey Mouse' is on the Brecon train but remains unidentified. The bracket signal is worthy of a second look!
Photograph: John Langford.

(*Above*) We have already mentioned the Mid Wales Line was affected with considerable falls of snow in its last week of operation. Despite this, the railway was able to run a normal timetable and so the public requiring to travel by train were least affected in the circumstances. I dare say that the buses found keeping to time on the local roads a little more difficult! As usual, the Brecon to Moat Lane service was running behind No.46516 and is seen here shrouded in steam in the freezing atmosphere at Talyllyn Junction. When the line closed the replacement bus services proved to be a disaster, and it took at least twelve months for those services to finally get their act together

Photograph: The late J. Fozard/S. Fozard

(*Above*) West of the station there was immediately Talyllyn Tunnel. This was built in 1816 for the Hay Railway (horse drawn) and was enlarged by the Brecon and Merthyr Railway and opened 1st May 1863. It was 674 yards long and passed under the Scethrog Ridge. A grimy looking No.46505 is arriving one June day in 1960. **Photograph**: D. J. Lowe Archive

(*Above*) At the opposite end of the station we see No.46513 in the 'extension platform', waiting for the 10.25am Brecon to Hereford connection which will stop in the station at the platform before the signal box. This will allow passengers to walk forward to this waiting train before continuing to Three Cocks Junction. Pannier Tank No.4611 meanwhile runs in with the 08.03am Newport to Brecon passenger train into the station. The date is 14th April 1962. **Photograph**: John Langford.

GROESFFORDD HALT

(*Left*) Looking westwards on a fine summers day in 1961 is Groesffordd Halt. Originally built by the GWR, it was opened on 8th September 1934 as part of the drive to attract walkers in the holiday season. A sleeper built platform on a wooden trestle system of supports, it also possessed the necessary corrugated shelter.
Photograph: The late J. Fozard/S. Fozard

(*Below*) The guard about to close the door of a stopping train. Note again how dependent the driver was on the guard as there is little visibility of the train itself as it stands in the platform.
Photograph: The late N. Jones/D. J. Lowe Archive

(*Left*) As we approach Brecon from the east, we pass Brecon Yard Ground Frame on our left where a signal box, formerly known as Hoel Lledron Junction once stood and where a line dropped down to the goods yard and engine shed. Here we see Pannier Tank No.8702 (an Ebbw Junction loco recently moved up from the West Country) having left Brecon on a Newport train in 1962 about to pass Brecon Yard GF. Over on the left part of the goods warehouse may be observed.

Photograph: D. J. Lowe Archive

(*Above*) A little further on we pass the coach sidings on the left which overlooked the lower yard (known as Watton Yard), containing the goods and locomotive servicing facilities. Also near here on the left we pass the former South Wales Borderers Barracks, now Regimental Museum of the Royal Welsh (Brecon). From the cab of No.46516 we can see Brecon Free Street station in the distance which we shall look at shortly. May 1962.

Photograph: The late N. Jones/D. J. Lowe Archive

Brecon MPD and Goods Yard
(incorporating former Watton Station)

'Main Line' To/From Talyllyn

Line joins 'Main Line' at 'Heol' former Lladron Junction

D. J. Lowe 2017

N

Coal Stack

Shunters Cabin

PW Hut

'Main Line' To/From Talyllyn

Headshunt from Brecon Station/Bay/Turntable Road

Mess Sand & Oil Store

Cattle Pens

Mess

Engine Shed

Platform

Loco Offices and Stores

Platform

Garage

Goods Warehouse

Main Coach Sidings

From Brecon Free Street Station

Weighbridge and Office

(Right) What was known as the 'Straight Siding' linked the lower Watton Yard with the 'joint' station at Brecon Free Street. April 1962.
Photograph: John Langford

(Left) A view of the old ex-B&M Watton platform and station buildings which were still utilised at this time as offices. May 1962. The line to the left is the start of the 'Straight Siding'.
Photograph: The late N. Jones/D. J. Lowe Archive

(*Above*) A fine Sunday morning in June 1960 at Brecon MPD sees a selection of motive power on shed. In the near foreground is 22XX Collett Goods No.2247, a former Worcester engine and now on the books of 86A Ebbw Junction. Behind are two unidentified 'Mickey Mouse' 2-6-0's whilst in the siding on the left lurks another 22XX 0-6-0 tender locomotive. The top of the locoshed may just be seen above the water tank which is behind the coaling shelter in the centre of the picture. The lack of steam from the shed indicates that other engines are either in light steam or out of use. Originally designated 89B, the shed became a sub shed to 89A (Oswestry) in 1959. In 1961, Oswestry was recoded to 89D which meant that several engines working the Mid Wales were seen with this code. However BR had other ideas and designated Brecon as being 88K! The staff incentive to carry out another recoding of engines, bearing in mind the iminent closure of the Mid Wales meant that no engines ever carried the 88K plates.

Photograph: D. J. Lowe Collection

95

(*Right*) At ground level, we see 22XX 0-6-0 No.2287 this time flanked by two Ivatt class 2's. The locomotives are standing on the old Cambrian shed road long since gone. The roof of the then current shed in use is just visible above the Collett tender. The GWR refurbished this shed in 1934. Around 10-15 engines were allocated here up until closure came on 31st December 1962, when all remaining passenger services to Brecon ceased. **Photograph**: D. J. Lowe Archive

BRECON
MPD

(*Centre below*) A steam line up at Brecon shed in the early 1960's. Engines featured are from right to left, No.46507 on the coal road, No.46515 infront of No.8751 in the main shed, No.2243, No.8766 and No.46523. **Photograph**: P. Fisher Collection

(*Left*) The early 1950's brought a new wave of locomotives to the Mid Wales Line, something that had long been wanting but was difficult to provide because of the axle weight restrictions. The improved Ivatt class 2's were the answer. Here we see No.46519 on shed at Brecon on 9th May 1953. The engine was in the all black lined out livery sporting the early BR lion on wheel ensignia on the tender. **Photograph**: P. Fisher Collection

(*Above*) This view shows the yard and goods facilities after the Mid Wales Line had been closed but when Brecon was still open for goods traffic for a while afterwards. It must be realised that the connection from Neath to Brecon had still been retained for goods traffic and this was used up until 4th May 1964. The picture shows 0-6-0 Pannier Tank No.9676 shunting freight into the goods shed on 2nd April 1963. Note the disused and dilapidated engine shed on the left. Soon Brecon would be left with no rail facilities at all

Photograph: Ben Ashworth

BR(WR) Brecon (Free Street)
(circa 1960)

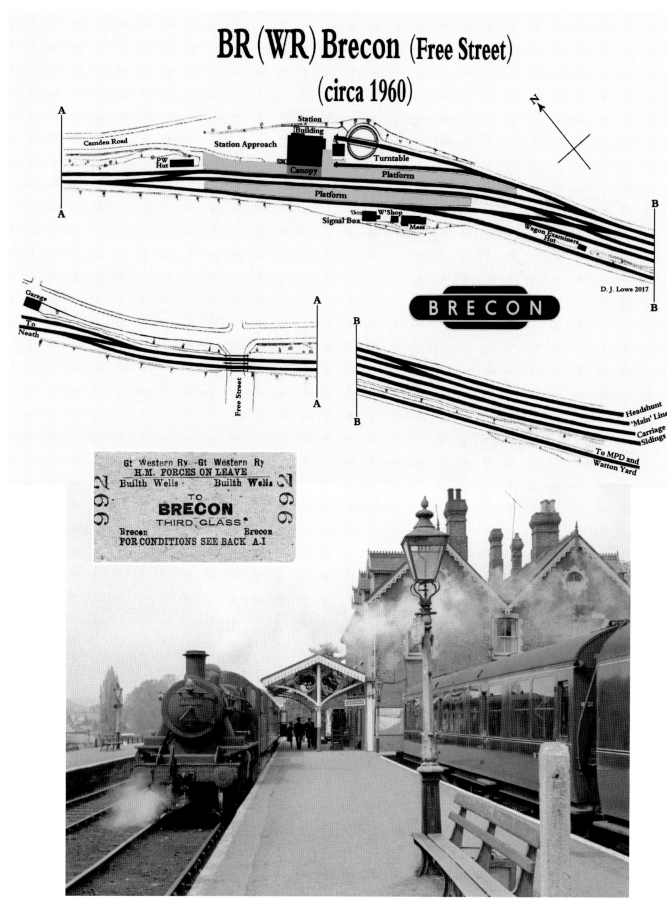

(*Above*) Brecon Free Street station, was owned by the B&M and used jointly, superseding earlier 'temporary' accommodation at Watton and Mount Street (further west along the Neath and Brecon line). Here we see No.46516 about to depart with the 1.20pm train for Moat Lane on 4th May 1962. **Photograph**: D. J. Lowe Archive

(*Above*) The station consisted of two through middle platform roads, the southern one on the left being an island platform. On the northern platform was sited the substantial three story brick building with a canopy running its full length. A bay platform was provided at the eastern end, used mainly for the Hereford service. Behind the bay was a turntable. On the left the replaced signal box of 1931 contained a 44-lever frame, the 'Straight Siding' running directly infront of it. No.46516 backs down onto its train in May 1962.
Photograph: D. J. Lowe Archive

(*Left*) In terms of railway infrastructure, little changed in the intervening years between this picture and the one above. Note that there was no protection for passengers on the island platform, not even a shelter! The authorities saw fit to erect a fence at the eastern end of the island platform to prevent passengers from falling off but not necessary at the end of the northern one! The Hereford train in the bay was being hauled by ex.LYR Aspinall class 27 No.52525 on 11th September 1951.
Photograph: The late H.C.Casserley
R.M Casserley

(*Left*) The turntable for some reason was positioned behind the bay platform at Brecon, and not down in the loco depot at Watton. The turntable was partially surrounded by a stone retaining wall as it was very close to the main road (Camden road) above. Here we see Pannier Tank No.4611 being turned by her crew on 14th April 1962. The engine had recently brought in a train from Newport and after watering and coaling at the depot would return shortly to Newport.
Photograph: John Langford

(*Below*) Ivatt class 2 No.46516 having just turned is seen picking its way off the turntable at Brecon on 4th May 1962.
Photograph: The late N. Jones
D. J. Lowe Archive

(*Above*) As we leave our train in the station we may perchance look back at Brecon station. This fine building was sadly demolished by the local authority on closure of the railway. Surely it could have been put to some use to benefit the local community? Perhaps it was too much to bear for some, losing all of its railway connections to be reminded of them by a building standing over the town? Here we see the station approaches in happier days in the late 1950's. A train stands in the platform on this lovely Spring day waiting to wind its way up the Mid Wales Line. The road off to the left is Camden Road and rose up slightly behind the station buildings and the turntable just here.

Photograph: P. Fisher Collection

WESTERN REGION

Day Excursion Bookings

EACH WEEKDAY

Commencing 12th June, 1961 and until further notice

TO

BRECON

FROM	DEPART a.m.	DEPART p.m.	DEPART SO p.m.	RETURN FARES (Second Class) s. d.
NEWBRIDGE-ON-WYE … … …	11 9	—	—	6/-
BUILTH ROAD (L.L.) … … …	11 19	12 30	—	5/3
BUILTH WELLS … … … …	11 25	1 20	4 18	5/-
ABEREDW … … … … …	11 34	1 30	—	4/3
ERWOOD … … … … …	11 40	1 35	4 29	3/9
LLANSTEPHAN HALT … … …	11 47	1 41	4 35	3/3
BOUGHROOD and LLYSWEN … …	11 52	1 45	4 40	2/9
BRECON … … … Arrive	p.m. 12 35	2 30	5 25	SO—Saturdays Only

Passengers may return by any Train Same Day affording a Service through to destination

Children under Three years of age, Free; Three and under Fourteen years of age, Half-fare. (Fractions of 1d. charged as 1d.)

IT WOULD ASSIST THE RAILWAYS IN PROVIDING ADEQUATE ACCOMMODATION IF INTENDING PASSENGERS WOULD OBTAIN THEIR TICKETS IN ADVANCE.

NO WORRY—NO STRAIN
MUCH BETTER BY TRAIN

CIRCULAR TOUR TICKETS FOR BUSINESS OR PLEASURE JOURNEYS AT REDUCED FARES.

Further information will be supplied on application to the Stations or to Mr. O. VELTOM, District Traffic Superintendent, Shrewsbury (Telephone Shrewsbury 3614, Extension 42); or Mr. W. R. STEVENS, Divisional Traffic Manager, Cardiff.

Paddington Station, W.2.
May, 1961.

R. HAMMOND,
General Manager.

No. 86 R.P. 20 — Printed in Great Britain by G. R. Griffith Ltd., Chester

Day excursion bookings from 12th June 1961 to Brecon

Table 185 MOAT LANE, LLANIDLOES, BUILTH ROAD, and BRECON

Week Days only

Miles	Station	a.m	a.m	a.m Saturdays only	a.m Except Saturdays	a.m Except Saturdays, or when Newtown School is closed	a.m	a.m Mondays only	a.m From Newport (Table 121)	a.m From Hereford (Table 144a)	a.m	a.m (From Newport (Table 121))	p.m	p.m Saturdays only From Hereford (Table 144a)	p.m	p.m	p.m From Newport (Table 121)	p.m From Hereford (Table 144a)	p.m	p.m	p.m Saturdays only	p.m (From Newport (Table 121))	p.m From Hereford (Table 144a)
	184 Whitchurch … dep	..	3 15	..	..	..	..	..	..	..	..	9 55	..	..	12S34	2 5	..	..	..	4 5	..	6 50	..
	184 Welshpool … "	..	4 45	..	..	..	..	..	..	..	9 0	1135	..	..	1S40	4 0	..	..	4 35	7 28	..	8 50	..
	184 Aberystwyth … "	..	..	..	..	..	..	..	..	..	7 10	9 55	..	..	12 50	2 30	..	..	2 30	6 0	..	..	..
—	Moat Lane Junc. … dep	..	5 45	..	..	8 30	..		..	..	9 55	1225	..	..	2 45	4 45	..	..	5 30	8 10	..	9 31	..
2	Llandinam …	..	5 50	..	..	8 35	..		..	..	10 0	1230	..	..	2 50	4 50	..	..	5 35	8 15	..	9 36	..
4¾	Dolwen …	..	5 56	..	..	8 41	..		..	..	10 6	1236	..	..	2 56	4 56	..	..	5 41	8 21	..	9 42	..
7½	Llanidloes … arr	..	6 2	..	..	8 45	..		..	..	1011	1242	..	..	3 2	5 2	..	..	5 46	8 27	..	9 47	..
	Llanidloes … dep	..	6 3	..	..		..		..	..	1015	—	..	..	3 3	..	..	..	5 50	..	8 30	—	..
10¾	Tylwch …	..	6 12	..	..		..		..	..	1023	Stop	..	..	3 12	..	..	..	5 59	..	8 39	Stop	..
12¼	Glan-yr-afon Halt …	..	..	..	..		..		..	..	1028	..	..	..	3 17	..	..	..	6 4	..	8 44	..	..
14¾	Pantydwr …	..	6 23	..	..		..		..	..	1035	..	..	..	3 23	..	..	..	6 10	..	8 51	..	..
16	St. Harmons …	..	6 27	..	..		..		..	..	1039	..	..		3 27	..	..	..	6 14	..	8 55	..	..
19	Marteg Halt …	..	..	..	..		..		..		1046	..	..		3 33	..	..		6 21	..	9 2	..	
21½	Rhayader …	..	6 39	..	..		..		..		1054	..	..		3 47	..	..		6 28	..	9 9	..	
24¾	Doldowlod …	..	6 46		..		..		..		11 1	..	..		3 54	..	..		6 40	..		..	
28¼	Newbridge-on-Wye …	..	6 54		..		..	9 52	..		11 9	..	..		4 2	..	..		6 50	..		..	
32¾	Builth Road (Low Level) arr	..	7 2		..		..	9 59	..		1117	p.m	..		4 10	..	..		6 58	..		..	
	Builth Road (Low Level) dep	6 30	7 5				9 10	10 0	..		1119	1225	..		4 11	..	..		6 59	..		..	
34¼	Builth Wells … arr	6 33	7 8				9 13	10 3	..		1122	1228	..		4 14	..	..		7 2	..		..	
	Builth Wells … dep	6 35	..				9 15	..	..		1125	—	1 10		4 16	..	..		7 5	..		..	
36¼	Llanfaredd Halt …	..	..				9 20	..	..		1130	Stop	1 15		4 22	..	..		Rr	..		..	
38¼	Aberedw …	6 44	..				9 24	..	..		1134		1 19		4 27	..	..		7 13	..		..	
41	Erwood …	6 50	..				9 30	..	..		1145		1 25		4 33	..	..		7 19	..		..	
43½	Llanstephan Halt …	..	..				9 36	..			1150		1 31		4 39	..	..		7 25	..		..	
45½	Boughrood and Llyswen	7 3	..			..	9 40	..		..	1155		1 36		4 44	..	..	..	7 30	..	..	..	..
48	Three Cocks Junc. arr	7 8	..			..	9 48	..		..	12 0		1 42		4 49	..	..	..	7 35	..	..	..	..
	Three Cocks Junc. dep	7 9	..	8 5	8 16	..	9 49	..		1033	12 2		1 43	1 54	4 50	..		5 19	7 36	..	..		10 5
50½	Talgarth …	7 18	..	8 11	8 22	..	9 55	..		1040	12 8		1 50	2 2	4 56	..		5 25	7 41	..	..		1012
53	Trefeinon …	7 25	..	8 18	8 30	..	10 1	..		1048	1214		1 57	Nn	5 3	..		5 36	7 49	..	..		Nn
54¾	Llangorse Lake Halt …	Bb	..	8 23	8 35	..	10 6	..		Aa	1219		2 2	Aa	Aa	..		Aa	7 54	..	..		Aa
56	Talyllyn Junction … arr	7 34	..	8 27	8 39	..	1011	..		1057	1226		2 6	2 13	5 12	..		5 42	7 59	..	..		1023
76	121 Merthyr … arr	9N4	..	..	..	..	..	..		..	1N40		3N32	..	..	..		7N45	..	..	..		..
99½	125 Cardiff B 131 … "	..	..	..	..	..	..	..	..	..	2Z43		4 51	..	..	..		..	..	..	..		..
98½	121 Newport … "	10 4	..	..	..	..	..	..	..	..	2 50		4 29	..	..	..		8 50	..	..	..		..
96½	121 Cardiff D … "	10 0	..	..	..	..	..	..	..	..	3T37	p.m	5 6	..	..	..		8 49	..	..	..	p.m	..
—	Talyllyn Junction … dep	7 47	..	8 29	8 40	..	1012	..	1041	11 2	1228	1 35	2 11	2 23	5 15	..	5 25	5 44	8 1	..	..	9 16	1025
58	Groesffordd Halt …	7 52	..	8 34	8 45	..	..	..	1046	..	1233	..	2 16	..	..	..	5 30	..	8 6	..	..	Rr	..
60	Brecon … arr	7 57	..	8 39	8 50	..	1021	..	1050	1110	1238	1 43	2 22	2 31	5 24	..	5 34	5 52	8 11	..	..	9 25	1033

Week Days only

Station	am	a.m	a.m Except Saturdays, or when Newtown School is closed	a.m	a.m To Hereford (Table 144a)	a.m To Newport (Table 121)	a.m Mondays only	a.m To Hereford (Table 144a)	a.m	p.m To Newport (Table 121)	p.m Saturdays only To Hereford (Table 144a)	p.m	p.m To Newport (Table 121)	p.m Except Saturdays	p.m	p.m To Hereford (Table 144a)	p.m To Newport (Table 121)	S
Brecon … dep	..	..	..	6 20	6 50	7 35	..	1032	1052	1215	1 10	1 20	2 0	4 15	5 5	6 5	6 15	9 35
Groesffordd Halt …	..	..	..	..	..	7 40	..	..	1057	1220	..	1 25	2 5	4 20	..	..	6 20	9 41
Talyllyn Junction … arr	..	..	..	6 29	6 59	7 45	..	1040	11 2	1225	1 18	1 30	2 10	4 25	5 14	6 13	6 25	9 46
121 Cardiff D … dep	..	..	..	..	..		..	8 15	8 15		..	10a55		..	2 40	..	..	6 53
121 Newport … "	..	..	..	..	..		..	8 3	8 3		..	11a0		..	3 0	..	..	6 55
125 Cardiff B 131 … "	..	..	..	..	..		..	7 40	7 40		..	10a35		..	2T15	..	..	6T34
121 Merthyr … "	..	..	..	..	..		..	9N28	9N28		..	12N10		..	4N10	..	..	8N0
Talyllyn Junction … dep	..	..	..	6 30	7 0		..	1042	11 3		1 22	1 33		4 26	5 25	6 14		9 47
Llangorse Lake Halt …	..	..	..	Kk	Gg		..	Gg	11 8		Gg	1 38		4 31	Kk	6 19		9 53
Trefeinon …	..	..	..	6 41	Gg		..	Gg	1113		Gg	1 43		4 36	5 35	Gg		9 59
Talgarth …	..	..	..	6 47	7 16		..	1058	1120		1 36	1 49	..	4 42	5 41	6 28		1011
Three Cocks Junc. arr	..	..	..	6 52	7 21			11 2	1125		1 42	1 54	..	4 47	5 46	6 34		1016
Three Cocks Junc. dep	..	..		6 53					1127			1 56	..	4 51	5 47			1017
Boughrood and Llyswen	..	..		7 5					1133			2 2	..	4 57	5 53			1023
Llanstephan Halt …	..	..		7 9					1137			2 6	..	5 1	5 57			1028
Erwood …	..	..		7 16					1145			2 13	..	5 8	6 4			1036
Aberedw …	..	..		7 22		—			1151	—		2 19	..	5 14	6 10		..	1042
Llanfaredd Halt …	..	..		7 27		Stop			1156	Stop		2 24	..	5 19	..		..	..
Builth Wells … arr	..	..		7 32		a.m			12 1	p.m		2 29	..	5 24	6 19		..	1051
Builth Wells … dep	..	..		7 37		8 55	9 35		12 5	1245		2 33	..		6 21		..	—
Builth Road (Low Level) arr	..	..		7 41	..	8 58	9 38		12 9	1249		2 37	..		6 25		..	Stop
Builth Road (Low Level) dep	..	..		7 42	..	..	9 39	..	—	1250		2 45	..		6 26	..	..	..
Newbridge-on-Wye …	..	..		7 50	..	..	9 47	..	Stop	1258		2 53	..		6 34	..	..	p.m
Doldowlod …	..	..		7 58	..	..	..	..	..	1 6		3 1	..		6 41	..	..	S
Rhayader …	..	..		8 5	..	..	..	..	..	1 15		3 9	..		6 50	..	..	9 20
Marteg Halt …	..	..		8 11	..	..	..	..	..	1 21		3 15	..		Rr	..	..	..
St. Harmons …	..	..		8 20	..	..	..	..	..	1 30		3 24	..		7 4	..	..	9 34
Pantydwr …	..	..		8 24	..	..	..	..	..	1 34		3 28	..	..	7 8	..	..	9 38
Glan-yr-afon Halt …	..	..		8 30	..	..	..	..	..	1 40	..	3 34	..	..	Dd	..	..	..
Tylwch …	..	..		8 34	..	..	..	..	..	1 45	..	3 38	..	..	7 18	..	..	9 46
Llanidloes … arr	..	..		8 43	..	..	..	..	a.m	1 53	..	3 46	..	..	7 27	..	..	9 54
Llanidloes … dep	630	7 10	8 5	8 46	..	..	..	..	1125	1 54	..	3 48	..	..	7 28	..	..	..
Dolwen …	635	7 15	8 10	8 51	..	..	..	..	1130	1 59	..	3 53	..	..	7 34	..	..	..
Llandinam …	640	7 21	8 15	8 57	..	..	..	..	1136	2 5	..	3 59	..	..	7 40	..	..	..
Moat Lane Junc. … arr	645	7 25	8 20	9 2	..	..	..	..	1140	2 9	..	4 4	..	..	7 45	..	..	..
184 Aberystwyth … arr	..	..	..	1145	..	..	..	..	2 11	..	..	6 0	..	..	9 42	..	..	..
184 Welshpool … "	724	8 8	..	9 45	..	..	..	..	1225	3 0	..	4 57	..	..	8 38	..	..	..
184 Whitchurch … "	911	..	..	12 3	..	..	..	..	2 39	4 34	..	7S51	..	..	1014	..	..	..

- a — a.m.
- Aa — Calls to take up on notice being given to the Station Master at Talgarth. Passengers wishing to alight must give notice to Guard at Talgarth
- B — Queen Street, via Merthyr
- Bb — Calls on Mondays only at 7 30 a.m. to take up passengers
- D — Queen Street, via Bargoed
- Dd — Calls on Wednesdays & Saturdays
- Gg — Calls to take up for Glasbury-on-Wye and beyond on giving notice to the Station Master at Talyllyn Junction
- H — Arr. 3 5 p.m. on Saturdays
- Kk — Calls to take up or set down. Passengers wishing to alight must give notice to Guard at Talyllyn Junction
- N — Third class only
- Nn — Calls to set down on notice being given to Guard at Talgarth
- Rr — Stops to set down on informing Guard at previous *stopping* Station

S or S Saturdays only — T Change at Pontypridd — Z Arr. 3 43 p.m. on Saturdays

Timetable for the line 30th June to 14th September 1952

Table 185 — **MOAT LANE, LLANIDLOES, BUILTH ROAD, HEREFORD and BRECON**
WEEK DAYS ONLY

Miles	Station	am	am	am		am	am	am	am	am	am	pm		pm	pm	am	pm	pm		pm	pm	pm	pm	pm		pm	pm	pm		pm	pm	pm	pm	pm	
	Notes					Except Saturdays and School Holidays				From Newport (Table 121)		From Newport (Table 121)					Except Saturdays and School Holidays			Saturdays only; From Newport (Table 121)			Saturdays only Commences 12th May, 1962; From Pontsticill (Table 121)			Except Saturdays		Saturdays only			From Newport (Table 121)	Saturdays only	Except Saturdays	Saturdays only	
	184 Whitchurch dep		3 15													9 45								2 5						4 10			6 50	6 50	
	184 Welshpool „		4 40								8 55					1125					3 35			4 40						7 15			8 45	1051	
	184 Aberystwyth „										7 35					1025		1235			2 30			2 30						6 0					
—	**Moat Lane** Junction dep		5 45			8 30					9 55					1227		2 50			4 45			5 27						8 3			9 26	1131	
2	Llandinam		5 50			8 35					10 0					1232		2 55			4 50			5 31						8 8			9 31	1137	
5	Dolwen Halt		dd			8 41					10 6					1238		dd			4 56			5 37						8 14			9 37	uu	
7¾	**Llanidloes** arr		6 2			8 45					1012					1244		3 5			5 2			5 45						8 20			9 42	1147	
	Llanidloes dep		6 5								1015							3 6						5 50											
11	Tylwch Halt		dd								1024							3 13						5 58											
12½	Glan-yr-afon Halt										1029							dd						6S 4											
14¾	Pantydwr		6 24								1035							3 30						6 10											
16¼	St. Harmons		dd								1039							3 33						6 15											
19	Marteg Halt										1046							dd																	
21½	Rhayader		6 42								1054							3 47						6 30											
24¾	Doldowlod		6 50								11 1							3 54						6 40											
29	Newbridge-on-Wye F		6 58								11 9							4 2						6 47											
32½	**Builth Road** arr		7 6								1117							4 10						6 55											
	(Low Level) dep	6 30	7 7				9 10	9 56			1119				1230			4 11						6 57			7 55								
34½	**Builth Wells** arr	6 33	7 10				9 13	10 0			1122				1233			4 14						7 0			7 58								
	Builth Wells dep	6 35					9 30				1125				1 20			4 18										8 0							
36½	Llanfaredd Halt						9 35				1129				1 25			dd										uu							
38½	Aberedw	6 44					9 39				1134				1 30			dd										uu							
41¼	Erwood	6 50					9 45				1140				1 35			4 29										8 12							
43½	Llanstephan Halt						9 51				1147				1 41			4 35										uu							
45½	Boughrood and Llyswen	7 0					9 57				1152				1 45			4 40										8 20							
—	Mls **Hereford** dep								9 2					1242								4 7				7 15						9 10			
—	5 Credenhill								9 13					1255								4 20													
—	9¼ Moorhampton								9 22					1 4								4 28										9 30			
—	12¼ Kinnersley								9 30					1 12								4 36				7 40						9 38			
—	14¼ Eardisley								9 36					1 17								4 42				7 45						9 45			
—	17½ Whitney-on-Wye								9 44					1 24								4 50				7 52						9 52			
—	21¼ **Hay-on-Wye**			7X55					9 54					1 34								5 1				8 5						10 5			
—	25¼ Glasbury-on-Wye			8X 2					10 2					1 43								5 9				8 12						1013			
48¼	**Three Cocks** Junction arr	7 7		8X 7			10 4		10 8		1159			1 48	1 52			4 47				5 14				8 17		8 24				1018			
	Three Cocks Junction dep	7 9		8 8					1012		12 0				1 55		4 30	4 50				5 18				8 20		8 25				1020			
50½	Talgarth	7 16		8 14					1017		12 6				2 1		4 38	4 56				5P30				8 25		8 31				1025			
53	Trefeinon Halt	7 23		8 20					1024		1213				dd		4 44	dd				dd				8 32		uu				aa			
54¾	Llangorse Lake Halt	7 30		8 24					1029		1218				dd		4 49	5 8				dd				8 37		uu				aa			
56	Talyllyn Junction arr	7 35		8 29					1033		1223				2 16		4 53	5 12				5P46				8 41		8 43				1037			
76	121 Merthyr arr																					7T47													
99½	125 Cardiff B „																					9S 2													
98½	121 Newport „	10 4									2 48				4 27							8S50													
96¾	121 Cardiff D 131 „	9 47									3n28				5 6							8S49													
—	Talyllyn Junction dep	7 47		8 31					1036	1046	1225	1 34			2 20		4 54	5 17		5 26		5P47	7 30			8 42		8 45			9Z13	1040			
58	Groesffordd Halt	7 52		8 35						1050	1230				2 25		4 58	dd		5 31		dd				8 46		uu			uu				
60	**Brecon** arr	7 57		8 41					1044	1055	1235	1 42			2 30		5 4	5 25		5 36		5P56	7 38			8 51		8 55			9Z22	1050			

aa Calls to take up on notice being given to the Station Master at Talgarth. Passengers wishing to alight must give notice to Guard at Talgarth
B Queen Street. via Merthyr
D Queen Street, via Bargoed
dd Calls if required on notice to Guard at previous *stopping* station or by giving hand-signal during daylight only
F 4½ miles to Llandrindod Wells Station
n On Saturdays arr 3 5 pm
P On Saturdays 4 minutes later
S Saturdays only
T Saturdays only and Second class only
uu Calls to set down on notice being given to Guard at previous *stopping* station
X Except Saturdays and School Holidays
Z On Saturdays 8 minutes later

Table 185—*continued* — **BRECON, HEREFORD, BUILTH ROAD, LLANIDLOES and MOAT LANE**
WEEK DAYS ONLY

Miles	Station	am	am	am		am	am	am		am	am	am		am	am		pm	pm		pm	pm	pm	pm	pm		pm	pm	pm	pm	pm		pm		pm	
	Notes							To Newport (Table 121)									To Newport (Table 121)					Except Saturdays and School Holidays	To Newport (Table 121)	Except Saturdays			Except Saturdays	Saturdays only		To Newport (Table 121); Saturdays only		Saturdays only Commences 12th May, 1962; To Bargoed (Table 121)		Saturdays only	
—	**Brecon** dep						6 50	7 35			8 15			1025			1210			1 20			2 5	4 10		5 5	6 0	6 0		6 15		8 30		9 35	
2	Groesffordd Halt							7 40			8 20			1030			1215			1 25			2 10	4 15		5 10	6 4			6 20				9 41	
4	Talyllyn Junction arr						6 59	7 45			8 25			1035			1220			1 30			2 15	4 20		5 15	6 9	6 8		6 25		8 39		9 46	
—	121 Cardiff D 131 dep													8 15						10a58						2S38								6 55	
—	121 Newport „													8 3						11a15						3S 0								6 55	
—	125 Cardiff B „													7T36												2S36									
—	121 Merthyr „													9N28												4S16									
—	Talyllyn Junction dep						7 0				8 30			1040						1 33				4 21		5C17	6 10	6 9						9 47	
5¼	Llangorse Lake Halt						dd				8 33			1044						1 37				4 24		dd	6 14	6 14						9 53	
7	Trefeinon Halt						7 9				8 38			1050						1 42				4 30		dd		dd						9 59	
9½	Talgarth						7 15				8 44			1055						1 48				4 36		5C32	6 23	6 23						10 6	
11¾	**Three Cocks** Junction arr						7 20				8 50			11 2						1 55				4 45		5C38	6 29	6 29						1012	
	Three Cocks Junction dep						7 22				8 51			11 6	1115					1 59	2 15			4 49		5 40		6 30						1020	
—	13¼ Glasbury-on-Wye						7 26							11 8							2 19			4 53				6 34							
—	17¼ **Hay-on-Wye**						7 36							1119							2 29			5 2				6 44							
—	21 Whitney-on-Wye						7 44							1128							2 37			5 11				6 53							
—	24¼ Eardisley						7 51							1136							2 44			5 18				7 1							
—	26 Kinnersley						7 56							1141							2 49			5 23											
—	29½ Moorhampton						8 3							1148							2 56														
—	32½ Credenhill						bb							1159							3 6														
—	38½ **Hereford** arr						8 27							1216							3 21			5 59				7 35							
14½	Boughrood and Llyswen										8 56				1120					2 4						5 46								1027	
16½	Llanstephan Halt										9 0				1126					2 11						dd								1032	
18¾	Erwood										9 7				1140					2 17						5 57								1040	
21¼	Aberedw										dd				1148					2 24						dd								1045	
23½	Llanfaredd Halt										dd				dd					2 28															
25½	**Builth Wells** arr										9 22				1158					2 32						6 12								1055	
	Builth Wells dep					7 45				8 55	9 40				12 5			1245		2 36						6 16			7 40						
27½	**Builth Road** arr					7 49				8 58	9 44				12 9			1249		2 42						6 20			7 44						
	(Low Level) dep					7 50												1250		2 48						6 22									
31	Newbridge-on-Wye F					7 58												1258		2 55						6 30									
35½	Doldowlod					8 5												1 6		3 2						6 38									
38½	Rhayader					8 13												1 15		3 10						6 48									
41	Marteg Halt					8 20												1 21		dd															
43¾	St. Harmons					8 29												1 30		3 24						7 0									
45½	Pantydwr					8 32												1 33		3 28						7 4									
47½	Glan-yr-afon Halt					8 39												1 38		dd						dd									
49	Tylwch Halt					8 43												1 42		3 37						dd									
52½	**Llanidloes** arr					8 51												1 50		3 46						7 21									
	Llanidloes dep	6 15	7 10	8 5		8 55						11 0						1 54		3 47		4 15				7 25									
55	Dolwen Halt	6 20	7 15	8 10		9 1						11 5						1 59		dd		4 19				dd									
58	Llandinam	6 25	7 21	8 15		9 6						1110						2 5		3 58		4 25				7 35									
60	**Moat Lane** Junction arr	6 29	7 25	8 20		9 12						1115						2 10		4 3		4 31				7 40									
103½	184 Aberystwyth arr					1136						2 10						5 45		7 25		7 25				9 30									
78½	184 Welshpool „	7 4	8 8			9 55						1158						2 55		5 0						8 35									
112½	184 Whitchurch „	9 0				1212						2 40						4 46		7S51						10 8									

a am
B Queen Street, via Merthyr
bb Calls to set down on notice to the Guard at Moorhampton and to take up on notice to the Station Master at Credenhill
C On Sats. dep Talyllyn Jn. 5 21 pm, Talgarth 5 34 and arr Three Cocks Jn. 5 39 pm
D Queen Street, via Bargoed
dd Calls if required on notice to Guard at previous *stopping* station or by giving hand-signal during daylight only
F 4½ miles to Llandrindod Wells Station
N Second class only
S Saturdays only
T Change at Pontypridd

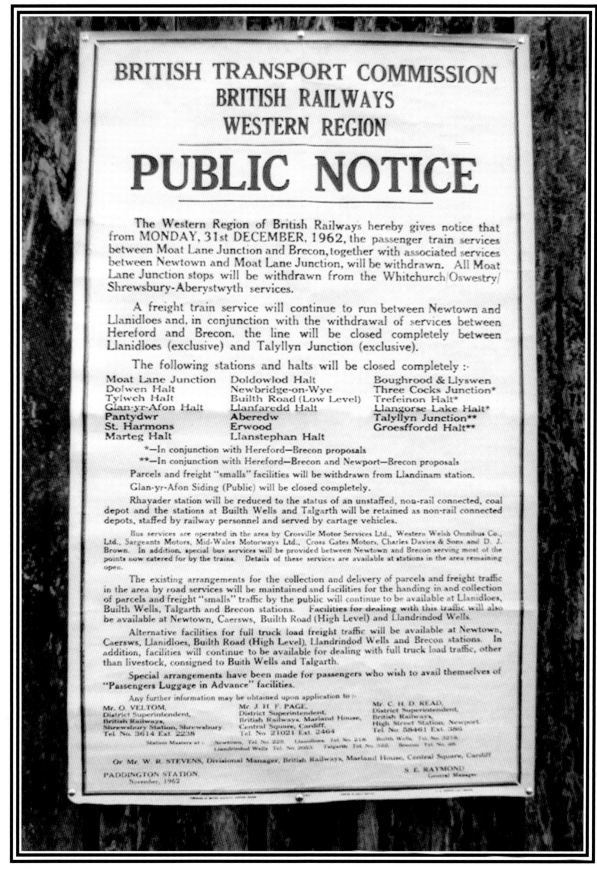

BRITISH TRANSPORT COMMISSION
BRITISH RAILWAYS
WESTERN REGION

PUBLIC NOTICE

The Western Region of British Railways hereby gives notice that from MONDAY, 31st DECEMBER, 1962, the passenger train services between Moat Lane Junction and Brecon, together with associated services between Newtown and Moat Lane Junction, will be withdrawn. All Moat Lane Junction stops will be withdrawn from the Whitchurch/Oswestry/Shrewsbury-Aberystwyth services.

A freight train service will continue to run between Newtown and Llanidloes and, in conjunction with the withdrawal of services between Hereford and Brecon, the line will be closed completely between Llanidloes (exclusive) and Talyllyn Junction (exclusive).

The following stations and halts will be closed completely :-

Moat Lane Junction	Doldowlod Halt	Boughrood & Llyswen
Dolwen Halt	Newbridge-on-Wye	Three Cocks Junction*
Tylwch Halt	Builth Road (Low Level)	Trefeinon Halt*
Glan-yr-Afon Halt	Llanfaredd Halt	Llangorse Lake Halt*
Pantydwr	Aberedw	Talyllyn Junction**
St. Harmons	Erwood	Groesffordd Halt**
Marteg Halt	Llanstephan Halt	

*—In conjunction with Hereford—Brecon proposals
**—In conjunction with Hereford—Brecon and Newport—Brecon proposals

Parcels and freight "smalls" facilities will be withdrawn from Llandinam station.

Glan-yr-Afon Siding (Public) will be closed completely.

Rhayader station will be reduced to the status of an unstaffed, non-rail connected, coal depot and the stations at Builth Wells and Talgarth will be retained as non-rail connected depots, staffed by railway personnel and served by cartage vehicles.

Bus services are operated in the area by Crosville Motor Services Ltd., Western Welsh Omnibus Co., Ltd., Sargeants Motors, Mid-Wales Motorways Ltd., Cross Gates Motors, Charles Davies & Sons and D. J. Brown. In addition, special bus services will be provided between Newtown and Brecon serving most of the points now catered for by the trains. Details of these services are available at stations in the area remaining open.

The existing arrangements for the collection and delivery of parcels and freight traffic in the area by road services will be maintained and facilities for the handing in and collection of parcels and freight "smalls" traffic by the public will continue to be available at Llanidloes, Builth Wells, Talgarth and Brecon stations. Facilities for dealing with this traffic will also be available at Newtown, Caersws, Builth Road (High Level) and Llandrindod Wells.

Alternative facilities for full truck load freight traffic will be available at Newtown, Caersws, Llanidloes, Builth Road (High Level), Llandrindod Wells and Brecon stations. In addition, facilities will continue to be available for dealing with full truck load traffic, other than livestock, consigned to Builth Wells and Talgarth.

Special arrangements have been made for passengers who wish to avail themselves of "Passengers Luggage in Advance" facilities.

Any further information may be obtained upon application to :-

Mr. O. VELTOM,
District Superintendent,
British Railways,
Shrewsbury Station, Shrewsbury
Tel. No. 3614 Ext. 2238

Mr. J. H. F. PAGE,
District Superintendent,
British Railways, Marland House,
Central Square, Cardiff.
Tel. No. 21021 Ext. 2464

Mr. C. H. D. KEAD,
District Superintendent,
British Railways,
High Street Station, Newport
Tel. No. 58461 Ext. 386

Station Masters at :- Newtown, Tel No. 226. Llanidloes, Tel. No. 218. Builth Wells, Tel. No. 3218. Llandrindod Wells. Tel. No. 2063. Talgarth. Tel. No. 322. Brecon. Tel. No. 66.

Or Mr. W. R. STEVENS, Divisional Manager, British Railways, Marland House, Central Square, Cardiff

PADDINGTON STATION,
November, 1962.

S. E. RAYMOND,
General Manager

(*Above*) End of the Line. I'm indebted to Mike Beach for providing me with this picture of the Closure Notice for the Mid Wales Line. It says it all really. We were now in the era of accountants for BR and Governments deciding whether railways stayed open or closed. Arguements were always loaded against retention. Whether it was important for local people and communities or not, money costs would decide in the end. It would be repeated many times over and accelerate even more once Dr Beeching and his Government paymaster Ernest Marples had initiated "The Reshaping of British Railways" in 1963.

Photograph: Mike Beach

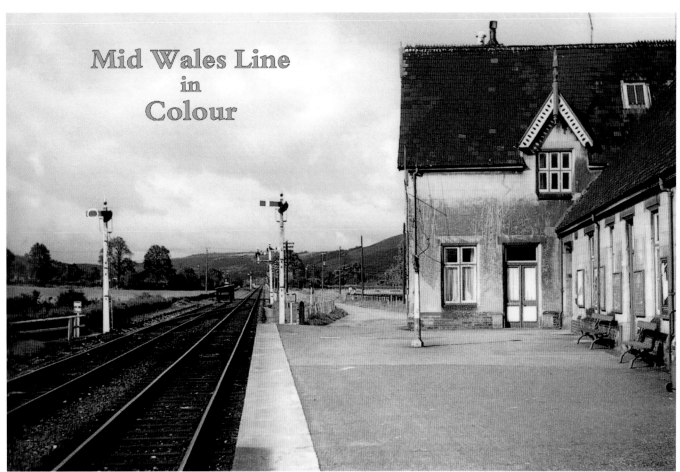

Mid Wales Line
in
Colour

(*Above*) A view from the Mid Wales platform at Moat Lane Junction looking south westwards towards Llanidloes and beyond in May 1961. The station approach can be seen leading away via a quite back lane to the main road. **Photograph**: D. J. Lowe Archive

(*Below*) The driver of No.46513 chats to his fireman as they take a breather in the loop at Moat Lane Junction on 31st March 1962. Some fine ex.GWR signals are on display including a ringed signal for shunting the loop headshunt. **Photograph**: John Langford.

BEWARE OF TRAINS

46513

(*Above*) By the late 1950's, the small shed at Moat Lane Junction was 'home' to four Ivatt class 2's and was a sub shed to Oswestry. In this late summers evening view we can see No.46521 simmering in the late sunshine with space available for a sister engine still out 'on the road'. This picture shows the 1957 shed which replaced the previous time spent one featured earlier in the book.
Photograph: D. J. Lowe Archive

(*Above*) A view c1960 sees the porter walking the platform at Llandinam. Note the abundance of railway posters here. At least nine Double Royal sized ones are on show in this view! Also of note are the attractive shrub and rose bushes along the platform. The wooden driveway across the tracks facilitated delivery vans picking up and collecting directly from the platform! **Photograph**: D. J. Lowe Archive

(*Above*) The imposing Llanidloes station, which fortunately has been saved and is in use today as business offices. It is the only surviving testment of the railway having once served the town. The original L&N station and yard (which was later abandoned despite still being shown on 1950 large scale O.S Maps!) was to the northeast of this second build. Note the south western wall is covered in tiles as a form of weather proofing. **Photograph**: P. Fisher Collection

(*Above*) In this colour view at Llanidloes it will be observed that the turntable road (right of No.46516) is rusty and not been used for some time. The turntable was 'recovered' (probably at a similar time to the one at Builth Wells.... December 1961?). Note also the small PW Trolley shed (right of signal box) no longer accessible because of the missing turntable. The coal wagon (right) still supplied the loco shed. 4th May 1962. **Photograph**: The late N. Jones/D. J. Lowe Archive

(*Above*) Looking down from the small overbridge at Tylwch on a lovely June morning in 1962. No.46505 and its two coaches make their way into the small halt, having just crossed over the Afon Dulas. The station and its adjoining buildings were of brick construction, with the old 'down' platform on the right by now well and truly grassed over, having been taken out of use in 1953. An engineers trolley siding is visible to the left of the engines front buffer beam. No.46505 will depart at 10.24am and take the ex.9.55am Moat Lane to Brecon train on its way southwards, providing a wonderful scenic journey for those lucky enough to be travelling on this fine day

Photograph: D. J. Lowe Archive

(*Above*) This is the daunting view of the line northwards out of Tylwch which crews faced and illustrates well the terrain that surrounded the small communtiy. Also of note (and rarely recorded), is the sign on the right. This sign told the driver that he was exiting from a zone of specially high fire risk. Of course he would have been warned of the commencement of the zone by seeing the slightly more familiar sign of a silhouette of a conifer tree on a yellow background sign. Such a sign is shown on page 39 and were introduced in 1959. In the distance the two bridges carry the line twice in close succession over the Afon Dulas. May 1962.

Photograph: The late N. Jones/D. J. Lowe Archive

(*Above*) On 22nd August 1959 John Langford took the 9.55am train from Moat Lane Junction to Brecon, his engine for the journey was No.46522. Here in the heart of Wales between Tylwch and Rhayader on a beautiful Summers day, the Mid Wales scenery puts on its very best for John who recorded this view from his carraige window. **Photograph**: John Langford

(*Above*) The small summit station at Pantydwr in the early 1960's sees the inevitable 'Mickey Mouse' No.46516 arrive with its train from Brecon. What is hard to appreciate is that from Three Cocks Junction to Pantydwr, (roughly 35 route miles), the train would have been faced with 27 miles of rising gradients, some as steep as 1 in 70, demanding the best from its engine crews. **Photograph**: D. J. Lowe Archive

St HARMONS
SIGNAL BOX

(*Left*) I've included this picture of St Harmons Signal Box to illustrate its small size and perhaps it might inspire some railway modeller to model it perhaps? Whether it was buildings or signals, it was structures like these that helped to give a line its character. A gatekeeper operated the crossing here but in latter days the train guard was responsible for operating the ground frame, which is what the box was then classified as. The siding on the other side of the crossing was accessed by a facing point from the direction of Rhayader on a gradient of 1 in 190 falling towards Rhayader. This meant that only 'down' trains could work the siding. This view was taken in May 1962 **Photograph**: D. J. Lowe Archive

(*Above*) Rolling under the Central Wales Line, Ivatt Class 2 No. 46523 brings its train to a halt at the Builth Road Low Level platform, having travelled down from Moat Lane on a lovely 14th April morning in 1962. The luggage lift is prominent on the right and looks to have been recently painted. **Photograph**: John Langford

(*Above*) A close-up of the luggage lift linking the Low Level with the High Level at Builth Road. The lift was restricted to raising or lowering 10 cwt. This was a rare structure at such a rural location and was in use until the Mid Wales Line was closed. **Photograph**: D. J. Lowe Archive

(*Above*) A view from the cab of No.46516 in 1962 at Builth Wells, and the gates are closed as we wait for our time for departure to Moat Lane. The stock in the distance are on the 'wagon repair siding' which was connected to the 'Welfield Siding' that lead to the CWS Milk Depot right. Note the AA kiosk, caravan and patrol motor bike also on the right!   **Photograph**: D. J. Lowe Archive

(*Above*) No.46523 waits at Builth Wells with the 9.10am from Builth Road to Three Cocks Junction on 14th April 1962. Services around Builth Wells were slightly more frequent than for any other station on the Mid Wales Line, as certain trains ran to connect with services on the Central Wales Line at Builth Road.   **Photograph**: John Langford

(*Above*) Trains go their own separate ways at Erwood. The northbound train in the platform is blowing off, the crew waiting for the signalman to lower the starting signal for it to proceed. In the small headshunt an elderly seven plank wagon resides, whilst on the right part of the cattle dock can be seen. 22nd August 1959. **Photograph**: John Langford

(*Above*) Llanstephan Radnor Halt in action! A passenger is dropped off at the small halt one April morning in 1962. The 'later' BR argument applied... did the passenger ticket cover the mechanical and coal consumption costs for stopping and starting from here? **Photograph**: John Langford

(*Above*) The peace and tranquility is broken at Three Cocks Junction as trains stand in the station having come in from three directions. The train on the left, hauled by No.46510 and partially hidden, is the 1.20pm train from Brecon, its final destination being Moat lane. Standing next to it is No.46523 in the 'down' platform with the 12.30pm Builth Road to Brecon passenger. In the 'up' Hereford platform on the right, No.46513 has already run round its train and marshalled its coaches waiting to depart with the 2.15pm service back to Hereford. A solitary covered van is in the goods yard on one of the loop sidings, while another siding ran along the back of the 'down' Hereford platform. Three Cocks Junction could well have become a triangular junction, the northern link running from the Mid Wales line to the Hereford line and though early excavations were made for this, the link-up was never made. **Photograph**: John Langford

(*Above*) This is the the engine on the 1.20pm Brecon to Moat Lane train referred to in our previous picture. Ivatt Class 2 2-6-0 No.46510 waits patiently in the 'up' 'Mid Wales' platform at Three Cocks Juntion on 14th April 1962. The signal is in the 'off' position and possibly the crew are waiting for our photographer to take their picture! The locomotive is one of the class that had the black lined livery applied after 1957 and like many of its brothers and sisters, would find further employment on remaining Cambrian lines after the Mid Wales Line closed. The tender looks to have adequate supplies of coal for its journey north, which is just as well, as most of the 35 mile route to Pantydwr will involve climbing! **Photograph:** John Langford

(*Above*) An Ivatt class 2 2-6-0 is held at the Inner Home signal on the North Curve at Talyllyn West Junction. The line from Newport/ Merthyr joins just ahead between the two telegraph poles in the centre of the picture. The later 'extension' platform of 1895 can be seen on the right and the public footpath also running parallel with the railway is roughly the line the early Hay Railway took before the coming of the railway proper. The latter used the original Talyllyn Tunnel of 1816 to access the Brecon & Abergavenny Canal. The end of the West Signal Box can be seen on the right with the main station buildings beyond. 14th April 1962. **Photograph**: John Langford

(*Above*) A lovely view of Talyllyn Junction on 22nd August 1959. Ivatt class 2 No.46522 in BR lined green livery is on a Mid Wales train, whilst in the other platform, an 0-6-0PT is being prepared to depart for Brecon with a train from Newport. Note the attached milk tank behind the three coaches which includes a very clean looking one in blood and custard livery. The West Junction Signal Box is worthy of note, especially how the brick edging and window surrounds compliments the colour of the stone. Note the wide walkway here to make access to and from the station easier for passengers. Great vigilance was needed at this point from the railway staff when passengers were required to change trains to travel onwards to their destinations.
Photograph: John Langford

(*Above*) Pannier Tank No.3767, now an 86A Newport engine but regular at Brecon for quite some years, has brought in its train from Newport. The driver stands and takes a breather at the end of the platform on this fine July afternoon in 1961. The brick built main station building dominates on the left. Note the platform side of the building had a rendered finish. Passengers accessed the island platform by having to use the walkway across the tracks as no footbridge was provided.   **Photograph**: D. J. Lowe Archive

(*Above*) Waiting to take out a Moat Lane Junction passenger train, Ivatt Class 2 No.46523 waits it's time at Brecon Free Street in August 1962. The signal box (designated Brecon Station) is to the left of the picture.   **Photograph**: D. J. Lowe Archive

(*Above*) The last public services to run on the Mid Wales Line were on Saturday 29th December 1962, there being no regular Sunday working on the line. However there was a special run by the Stephenson Locomotive Society on Sunday 30th December, to commemorate the closure of all lines radiating out of Brecon. It comprised of ten coaches and was double headed by two Ivatt Class 2 locomotives, Nos 46504 and 46509. The train is seen here at Llanidloes where a stop was made before continuing on its way south. It was touch and go whether the train would be allowed to run because of the snow, but in the end the authorities relented and permission was granted. After the thaw the lines were silent and 170 route miles including those of the Mid Wales, were consigned to scrap. Whilst some railwaymen were redeployed, many were made redundant and were forced to look for other jobs. Wales had lost one of its north to south links, it would not be its last!

Photograph: D. J. Lowe Archive

2nd - SPECIAL ARRANGEMENT
STEPHENSON LOCOMOTIVE SOCIETY
(MIDLAND AREA)
LAST PASSENGER TRAIN.
Moat Lane—Brecon. Brecon—Hereford
SUNDAY 30th DECEMBER. 1962
Shrewsbury, Welshpool, Moat Lane,
Llanidloes, Rhayader, Builth Wells, Three
Cocks Junction, Talyllyn Junction, Brecon,
Hay-on-Wye, Eardisley, Hereford,
Moorfields, Leominster, Shrewsbury
(W)   (8392)   For conditions see over